CULTURES OF THE WORLD
Grenada

Cavendish
Square

New York

GRENADA TODAY

SOMEONE SEARCHING THE WORLD FOR A TROPICAL ISLAND paradise might just choose Grenada (gre-NAY-dah). The "Spice Isle," as it's called, has breathtaking sandy beaches and a lush countryside fragrant with nutmeg-scented air. Spices have long been grown here—most famously nutmeg, but also cinnamon, cloves, and ginger—hence the nickname. The tropical climate also yields abundant fruits and vegetables, and the clean ocean waters provide a wealth of seafood. Not least of all, Grenada's cocoa industry produces some of the world's best chocolate. That alone may qualify the island as paradise!

This potential candidate for heaven-on-earth is an independent nation made up of three main inhabited islands—one larger island (Grenada), plus the smaller islands of Carriacou and Petite Martinique. They are among the hundreds of Caribbean islands, which as a group are called the West Indies. Within that category, Grenada is one of the Lesser Antilles, a chain of small volcanic islands in the North Atlantic Ocean that arc northward from off the coast of Venezuela. While probably any one of these tiny islands could qualify as paradise, Grenada has attributes that make it stand out. Compared to some of the others, it's said to be less developed as a playground for

A young woman sells spices from her colorful market stall in Saint George's, the capital of Grenada.

the rich and more authentic as a place where "real" people live and work. Nevertheless, where spices once ruled the economic roost, tourism has become the nation's most important industry.

Grenadians have a reputation for being friendly and welcoming. They are mostly the descendants of enslaved African people brought to the islands centuries ago to work the sugarcane plantations. Today, their lifestyles are imbued with a typical laid-back Caribbean vibe—an easygoing way that is evident in their festive music, dance, carnivals, and other traditions.

Most Grenadians are far from wealthy. In fact, poverty is a serious problem for this tiny nation. Grenada has one of the highest unemployment rates in the Caribbean, with about 24 percent of people without work in 2017. According to the World Bank, 32 percent of Grenada's 107,000 people are considered poor, and 13 percent live in extreme poverty. The poorest people live in the rural parts of the small country, away from the tourism-driven mainstream economy.

Many young people are choosing to move away from farming and agricultural work to work in the tourism industry, which tends to pay better. However, what Grenada's youth really need are not simply jobs, but better education and the professional skills necessary for building strong, sustainable careers.

With that in mind, the government launched a new initiative in 2018 aimed at reducing rural poverty and youth unemployment. The Climate-Smart Agriculture and Rural Enterprise Programme, SAEP, partly funded by the Caribbean Development Bank, aims to increase agricultural production and sustainability for farmers and other vulnerable groups in rural communities. It provides farmers with information about how to adapt to climate change in order to build sustainable livelihoods, and focuses on supporting start-up

A cocoa farmer smiles for the camera.

and existing businesses in rural areas. The program expects to benefit some 7,400 individuals, with about 4,400 of them being youth and women who head their own households.

The emphasis on climate change is important. Grenada is very concerned about how global warming will affect island life, and it is already seeing these climate effects in action. Grenada has always been vulnerable to hurricanes, but extreme weather events are increasing in scale and quantity. In 2004, Hurricane Ivan hit Grenada dead on, causing unprecedented devastation. Having struggled back from that catastrophe, the government knows all too well the importance of being better prepared to withstand severe weather.

Other climate change effects, such as rising oceans, will wreak havoc on any small island nation without some plan in place. The Caribbean is the most

Beach chairs beckon on a white sandy beach in Grenada. In the background, a cruise ship pulls into harbor.

tourism-dependent region in the world. Beach erosion—and indeed, complete beach submersion as sea levels rise—will surely undermine tourism, causing incredible economic hardship to the islands. Rising ocean temperatures will impact sea life, disrupting fisheries and adding to food insecurity. Rising temperatures on land and changing rainfall patterns will affect the kinds of crops that can be grown. As temperatures rise, epidemics of tropical diseases will increase as the carrier mosquitoes increase in density.

With these concerns in mind, Grenada hosted the Third Global Conference on Climate and Health for the Caribbean region in 2018. Organized by the World Health Organization (WHO) and the Pan American Health Organization, the conference highlighted the need for Caribbean leaders to build climate-resilient health systems.

Poverty and climate change are only some of the challenges facing Grenada, but they are among the most important. With such hurdles to leap, the island nation might not be everyone's idea of paradise after all. However, to the folks who live there, this land of incomparable beauty, extraordinary culture, and smiling people is home.

Grenadians don colorful traditional dress to perform at festivals and for tourists.

GEOGRAPHY

**Grand Anse Beach in December is
a welcoming destination.**

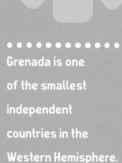

1

L YING ABOUT 100 MILES (160 kilometers) north of Venezuela is the tiny island nation of Grenada. It's part of an archipelago of more than seven thousand islands in the Caribbean Sea, many of them nothing more than little rocky outcrops poking above the surface of the ocean.

The nation of Grenada is made up of three main islands: Grenada, Carriacou, and Petite Martinique. The island of Grenada itself is about 21 miles (34 km) long and 12 miles (19 km) wide at its widest. Carriacou lies 23 miles (37 km) northeast of Grenada Island. Petite Martinique is another 2.5 miles (4 km) northeast of Carriacou. The three main islands have a total landmass of 133 square miles (344 square kilometers). In addition, there are more than twenty very small islands and cays. The island of Grenada is 120 square miles (311 sq km), about twice the size of Washington, DC, while Carriacou is 13 square miles (34 sq km), and Petite Martinique is 486 acres (197 ha).

THE CARIBBEAN ISLANDS

The Caribbean islands lie south of Florida, separating the Caribbean Sea to the west from the Atlantic Ocean to the east. The largest islands in the group—Cuba, Jamaica, Hispaniola, and Puerto Rico—make up the Greater Antilles. North of these four large islands are the many islands of the Bahamas.

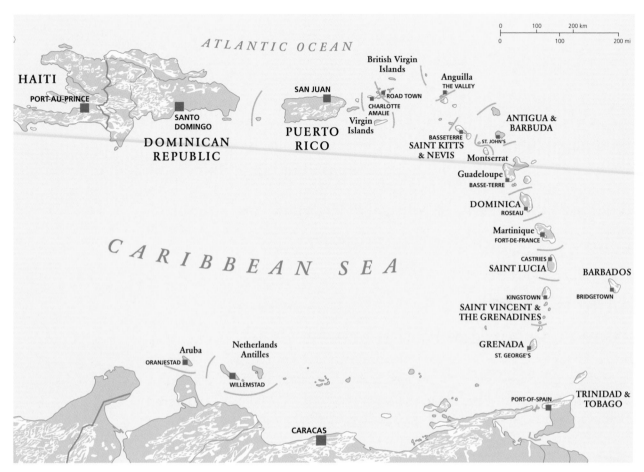

The islands of the Lesser Antilles lie to the east and south of Puerto Rico. The Lesser Antilles are divided into two groups: the Leeward Islands and the Windward Islands. The Windward Islands are Dominica, Martinique, Saint Lucia, Saint Vincent, Barbados, the Grenadines, and Grenada, while the Leeward Islands include those between Anguilla and Guadeloupe and their adjacent islands. Finally, there is a group of islands closest to the Venezuelan coast: Trinidad and Tobago, Aruba, Bonaire, and Curaçao.

Geologists believe that during the last ice age, all the Caribbean islands formed a land bridge that linked Florida with Venezuela. This landmass was then submerged by the sea in a series of earthquakes and volcanic eruptions so that only the tops of the mountains remain above water, as islands.

This map shows the Caribbean Sea, with some islands of the Greater Antilles to the north, and the islands of the Lesser Antilles to the east. To the south is the northern coast of Venezuela, with its capital of Caracas.

BALMY ALL YEAR

Lying south of the Tropic of Cancer, Grenada has a warm climate year-round. The average daily temperature is 81 degrees Fahrenheit (27 degrees Celsius), and this does not vary much throughout the year. The coolest months are from December to March, and the hottest are from August to November. There is a greater difference in temperature throughout the day, as daytime temperatures can hit above 86°F (30°C), falling to the low 70s°F (low 20s°C) at night. Although the Caribbean islands are in the hurricane belt, Grenada has, in general, been less affected than other islands by these destructive winds. However, many heavy thunderstorms still pass over Grenada during the hurricane season.

RAINFALL

Grenada has wet and dry seasons. The dry season is from January to May, when the hills turn brown due to lack of rain and rivers are low. The heaviest rainfall occurs from June to December, making the land green once again.

The highest rainfall occurs in the central mountains and in the sheltered valleys on the windward side of the mountains. These receive an average of 160 inches (406 centimeters) a year. The coastal regions are drier, getting about 50 inches (127 cm) a year, especially on the leeward side of the island. The southern tip is the driest part of the island. Grenada also receives convectional rain. This occurs when the land heats up during the day. This heats the air, which rises and creates a powerful updraft. As the air rises, it cools, and the moisture it contains is released as rain that often falls in the mid-afternoon.

TOPOGRAPHY

Like the other Windward Islands, Grenada has a rich and varied terrain. There are high mountains, rain forests, deep river valleys, beautiful lakes, some desert-like areas, strings of beautiful white-sand and black-sand beaches, and deep, sheltered harbors.

HURRICANES

Hurricanes are a significant climatic phenomenon in the Caribbean. In the summer, strong winds develop in troughs of low pressure in the Atlantic Ocean and eastern Caribbean, bringing unsettled, overcast weather, often accompanied by heavy rains. Sometimes these winds gather enough force to become a hurricane.

"Hurricane" comes from a Carib word, huracan *(HU-rah-cahn). It refers to a tropical storm with heavy rain and winds that exceed 74 miles per hour (119 kilometers per hour). These high-velocity winds blow in a counterclockwise direction around a low-pressure center, known as the eye of the storm, where the winds are calm. Yet the strongest winds rage most fiercely at the points closest to the eye. As the hurricane roars through, the area affected by the storm may be more than 150 miles (241 km) wide. The hurricane season is from June to November, with the most frequent occurrences in August and September. On average, about five to eight hurricanes develop a year, but many fizzle out before they reach land.*

The most destructive hurricane in the island's recorded history was Hurricane Ivan, which hit Grenada on September 7, 2004. It killed thirty-nine people and damaged or destroyed 90 percent of the island's homes and buildings.

The highest peak is Mount Saint Catherine, which is 2,757 feet (840 meters) high. Other mountains on the island—Mount Granby, Mount Lebanon, and Mount Sinai—rise more than 2,000 feet (610 m) above sea level. A number of rivers begin in the central mountains and flow to the sea.

Grenadians may call the same river by many names, depending on which part of the country or which village it passes through. Major rivers include the Great River, which flows through the parish of Saint Andrew, Saint John's River, and Saint Patrick's River.

LAKES AND BEACHES

There is much evidence on Grenada Island, especially on the north coast, of previous volcanic activity—volcanic vents, black-sand beaches, and sulfurous springs. Several extinct volcanic craters are now filled with beautiful lakes, such as Levera Pond and Lake Antoine in the northeast, and Grand Etang Lake in the center of the island.

Grand Etang Lake is 1,700 feet (518 m) above sea level. The area around it is a national park and a forest reserve. The park can easily be reached by road and by paths that allow visitors to enjoy the thick natural rain forest that surrounds the crater. Lake Antoine is just 20 feet (6 m) above sea level, and it is 16 acres (6 ha) in size. It was formed twelve thousand to fifteen thousand years ago during Grenada's final stage of volcanic activity.

The Grenadian coastline, which stretches for more than 80 miles (129 km), is indented by many beautiful bays and lovely beaches. The two most spectacular beaches are on the southern tip of the island—Lance aux Epines and the Grand Anse.

Grand Etang Lake, in the national park of the same name, is a crater lake in an extinct volcano. The lake is about 20 feet (6 m) deep and about 36 acres (14.5 ha) in area. It is featured on Grenada's coat of arms.

RAIN FORESTS

There is a wide variety of natural vegetation on Grenada Island—lush tropical rain forests, woodlands, mangrove swamps, and desert scrubland. Tropical rain forests flourish on the windward side of the mountains. Trees that grow more than 100 feet (30 m) tall are covered with mosses and ferns. Seasonal rain forests grow in slightly drier areas. They originally covered most of the lowland regions and can still be found on the leeward side of the island.

Dry forests grow in regions that receive between 30 and 50 inches (76 and 127 cm) of rain a year. Trees that grow here are rarely more than 30 feet (9 m) tall, and they lose their leaves in the dry season. Where people have cleared the forests, they have left flat, dry savannas with scrub trees. Thorny trees and cacti grow on the dry leeward coasts. Mangrove swamps, trees, and shrubs that can survive in shallow and muddy salt water cover some coastal areas.

FLORA

The tropical climate supports a vast number of economically useful trees. Fruit trees such as mango, papaya, and soursop are grown everywhere. There are palm trees of many kinds—date palms, queen palms, royal palms, and coconut palms. The coconut palm is extremely useful; it provides food, drink, oil for cooking, and building materials. Other common trees are the banyan, the mahogany, and the calabash. Banyans are large trees with spreading branches and

A bougainvillea plant blooms on a sunny day in Saint George's.

roots that hang from the branches to the ground. The mahogany, a native of the Caribbean, is valued for its wood. Calabash trees have large round fruit with hard shells that can be hollowed out and made into bowls, utensils, and craft objects. Beautiful flowering plants, including orchids, gingers, hyacinths, bougainvilleas, hibiscuses, allamandas, frangipani, and oleanders, are found everywhere. The bougainvillea is Grenada's national flower.

FAUNA

When the Europeans arrived in the fifteenth century, they discovered limited animal life because few animals had been able to cross the water from South America. They did find bats and rodents, including hutias—large, edible animals that reminded the Spanish of rabbits. The mongoose is commonly found in Grenada. It was brought by sugarcane farmers to help get rid of the cane rat. However, the mongoose, being a daytime hunter, was not much help in killing the nocturnal rat. Instead, it became a nuisance, preying on other small island animals.

There are several varieties of reptiles, including caimans, snakes, and lizards. Iguanas, which can grow to 5 feet (1.5 m) or more in length, are hunted by some who consider them a delicacy. However, the iguana has fallen prey to the mongoose. There are no poisonous snakes on the island. Troops of mona monkeys, introduced from West Africa centuries ago, live in the forested areas.

There are many kinds of birds, butterflies, and insects. The Grenada dove is Grenada's national bird. It lives only in Grenada and is critically endangered. In 2018, there were 110 doves left on the island, with the population in decline. Other birds commonly found in Grenada include bananaquits, hummingbirds, swifts, wrens, flycatchers, thrushes, finches, and blackbirds. The island is a welcome stop for thousands of other birds on their migratory route from the north.

The seas are rich in marine life. The tropical fish are plentiful and colorful. There are groupers, snappers, angelfish, parrot fish, wrasses, and other reef inhabitants. Sea turtles come ashore from March to August to lay their eggs. There are several species: green turtles, leatherbacks, loggerheads, olive ridleys, and hawksbills. Turtles are sometimes sold in the fish markets because some people love to eat turtle meat, but hunting laws protect them during certain times of the year.

A critically endangered Grenada dove (*Leptotila wellsi*), Grenada's only endemic bird, stands in the scrubby woodlands that make up its habitat.

FRENCH-BUILT TOWNS

The capital of Grenada is Saint George's (also written St. George's), which is on the south end of the island on a peninsula about 1 mile (1.6 km) long. About 7,500 people live in the city proper, but with workers from other parts of the island, as well as tourists, the population is actually much higher. The city's almost landlocked harbor, which is the crater of an extinct volcano, is so sheltered and deep that huge ocean liners are able to dock there.

The waterfront, known as the Carenage, has pink, ocher, and brick-red commercial buildings and warehouses, many dating from the eighteenth century. The town was designed by a former French governor, De Bellair de Saint-Aignan, in 1705, and planning was continued by the British when they

Grenada has a few pristine natural areas that have been preserved. The Levera National Park on the northeast coast has dry woodland vegetation and a saltwater lagoon with a white-sand beach. The lagoon is sheltered by coral reefs with mangrove swamps on either side. La Sagesse Nature Center along the southeast coast has mangroves, coral reefs, and dry woodlands.

The largest national park on Grenada is the Grand Etang National Park, which covers the most mountainous central region of the island. Mount Saint Catherine, Grenada's highest mountain; Mount Qua Qua; and Mount Fedon are the jewels of the park. Grand Etang Lake, which is in the crater of an extinct volcano, is a 36-acre (14.5 ha) expanse of beautiful water. Visitors can hike in the park using the many nature trails that have been developed.

The Caribbean Sea off the coast of Saint George's can be seen from Grand Etang National Park.

took control of the island. A ridge divides Saint George's into two parts that are joined by the Sendall Tunnel, a 10-foot-wide (3 m) tunnel constructed in 1894.

Gouyave, the second-largest town, with a population of 3,380, is the main town of Saint John Parish. Many of the residents make their living from fishing. It is surrounded by nutmeg estates, and the nutmeg processing station is the town's largest building.

Grenville, an agricultural town with a population of about 2,475, is the third-largest town in Grenada and the main port on the east coast. It is a regional center for collecting cocoa, nutmeg, and other agricultural products. It was established in 1763 by the French, who called it La Baye. Victoria Street, the main street facing the waterfront, is the focus of the town's activity.

The red roofs and white buildings of the Carenage section of Saint George's make for a colorful harbor view.

HISTORY

An old cannon points to the sea at historical Fort George in Saint George's.

2

G RENADA'S HISTORY STRETCHES back to a time long before Christopher Columbus arrived in 1492. Many centuries earlier, the Arawak people came from the mainland of South America and settled there. Over the years, three main groups of indigenous peoples, or Amerindians, came to the island.

• • • • • • • • • • • • •

Grenada was formed about two million years ago by an underwater volcano. No one is sure exactly when the first people arrived, but it might have been as early as five thousand years ago.

The first Grenadians were the little-known Ciboneys, who may have migrated south from Florida, Cuba, and Hispaniola thousands of years ago. Their name, meaning "stone people," was given to them by the next group of people who arrived, the Arawaks. A peaceful people, the Arawaks lived mostly on fish and cassava. Their petroglyphs can be seen in northern Grenada. A fierce and warlike group of Amerindians arrived next. They raided Arawak villages, killed the men, and enslaved the women. When the Europeans arrived there, they called these people Caribs, and the area came to be known as the Caribees. From this comes the name Caribbean.

GRENADA ON THE MAP

The Caribbean was first placed on the map in 1492 when, in the employ of the Spanish, the Italian adventurer Christopher Columbus spotted the Bahamas, specifically what is now called San Salvador. Columbus was searching for a westward passage to the East Indies. He explored the Bahamas and the north coast of Cuba before reaching the northeastern tip of another large island that he named Isla Española, known today as

Hispaniola. Leaving some men behind to establish a small settlement, Columbus returned to Spain to report his discovery.

In 1498, on his third trip to the Caribbean, Columbus arrived at the north of Grenada, then called Camerhogne by the Amerindians. He named the island Concepción. The name was changed to Granada on the sixteenth century maps, perhaps because the green hills reminded the Spanish sailors of Granada in Spain. No one is sure. The French, who settled on the island in the 1600s, changed the name to Grenade. When the British took possession of the island in 1763, the island came to be known as Grenada.

THE LURE OF GOLD

Columbus's exciting discovery of previously unknown (to Europeans) lands opened the floodgates of European exploitation. Over the next few centuries, the Caribbean islands were pawns in a game of power among the Spanish, the French, the British, and the Dutch.

Spain's interest was centered primarily on the islands of Cuba, Jamaica, and Puerto Rico, as gold could be found on them. Native people were forced to work in the gold mines until the gold was exhausted. The Arawak population was decimated, while the Caribs survived by retreating to the mountainous interiors and fighting back with some success.

When more gold was discovered in Peru and Mexico, the islands lost their importance. Nonetheless, Spanish ships were still attacked by English and French pirates. The Dutch entered the fray later. They wanted the high-grade salt of Venezuela and tobacco, which was becoming popular in Europe.

After years of plundering Spanish possessions, the northern Europeans established their colonies in the Caribbean in the 1600s. Possession of the islands changed hands according to the fortunes of war in Europe.

EARLY COLONIZATION

The first colonies were run by merchants authorized by their governments to represent them. When the islands became economic burdens, the French government sold them to the merchant governors.

The Caribs resisted early colonization attempts by the Europeans. In 1650, two Frenchmen bought Saint Lucia, Grenade, and the Grenadines. Hostilities soon broke out. Three years later, the French governor of Guadeloupe sent a force to Grenade that overran and killed the Caribs, finally cornering the last few in the north of the island. Rather than surrender, the remaining forty Carib men, women, and children leaped off a cliff to their deaths. The cliff is now called Leapers' Bluff.

The island continued to change hands during the next two decades. After the Treaty of Utrecht in 1713 that ended the War of the Spanish Succession, the Caribbean enjoyed almost eighty years of peace and prosperity.

BRITAIN WINS GRENADA

In 1762, the British fleet sailed for Grenade and took it easily without even firing one shot. They promptly renamed the island Grenada. This victory was formalized in 1763 by the Treaty of Paris. This treaty also gave Britain control over Saint Vincent, Dominica, and Tobago.

Thousands of adventurers from the British Isles immediately sailed for the Caribbean. They cleared the forests, planted sugarcane, built sugar mills, and imported thousands of captured and enslaved people from Africa.

The new sugar plantations thrived on Saint Vincent and Grenada until 1795, when they were devastated by slave rebellions. In 1779, when the British fleet left the Caribbean to accompany some merchant ships to Britain, the French captured Saint Vincent. They sailed for Grenada and repossessed it after a two-day battle, but under the Treaties of Versailles signed in 1783, Grenada once again returned to British hands.

SLAVES AND REVOLTS

During the French occupation, the British settlers were treated badly. So when the British regained control, the French suffered before eventually rebelling in 1795. Led by Julien Fedon, a Grenadian planter of African and French ancestry, thousands of slaves and "free coloreds" had the British on the run for more than a year.

Prime Minister Maurice Bishop holds a press conference in the 1980s.

ruthless dictator who brutally silenced his detractors. He employed a contingent of secret police called the Mongoose Gang to terrorize his political opponents. Gairy came to believe he was a messiah sent by God to rule Grenada and was known to say, "He who opposes me opposes God."

In 1979, while Gairy was in New York addressing the United Nations, a group of armed rebels overthrew him in a bloodless coup. Their leader, Maurice Bishop (1944–1983), became the prime minister of the new People's Revolutionary Government of Grenada. Bernard Coard, the deputy leader, became the minister of finance. Bishop's early rule saw an improvement in the lives of Grenadians.

Influenced by Cuban president Fidel Castro, Bishop adopted a communist-style government. He suspended the constitution and invited Cuban advisers to Grenada. He clamped down on press freedom, and the prison was packed with political prisoners. His communist alignments made the United States and other Caribbean nations very uneasy. At the same time, there was a struggle for power between Bishop and the more left-wing members of his party.

In October 1983, the hard-liners under Coard's leadership mounted a military coup and put Bishop under house arrest. Thousands of Bishop's supporters gathered at Fort George to demand his release. The army opened fire on the crowd and killed about forty people. Bishop and seven associates and advisers were then taken out and executed. The government imposed a four-day curfew with orders to shoot on sight anyone found on the streets without permission.

At a meeting of the Organization of Eastern Caribbean States (OECS), it was agreed that US help should be sought. The United States was all too happy to oblige, having been concerned about Bishop's close relationship with Castro, who the US considered an enemy.

THE SIX-DAY INVASION

On October 25, 1983, at the request of the governor-general, a combined force of the OECS and nearly six thousand US troops invaded Grenada. Ronald Reagan,

Several conditions precipitated the action of the United States and the OECS against Grenada. After the assassination of Maurice Bishop, the military council took control of the island, but there was utter chaos in the streets. The United States was also concerned that the Cuban-built Point Salines International Airport (now called the Maurice Bishop International Airport) would be put to military use, with Grenada becoming a missile base for the Cubans. The presence of some American medical students studying at Saint George's Medical School provided the needed excuse, and the invasion was ordered on the strength of protecting these students from the unstable situation.

On October 25, 1983, twenty-one helicopters from the US aircraft carrier Guam *landed on the beach near Pearls Airport on the eastern side of the island. There was token resistance and anti-aircraft fire, but this was quickly silenced. Another landing of helicopters farther south near the town of Grenville was met with little resistance. Some Grenadians waved to the invading forces and welcomed them as liberators. By October 31, the Americans had gained complete control of the island, and the six-day war was over. Some members of the People's Revolutionary Government escaped, but most of them voluntarily surrendered.*

American students board a C-141B Starlifter aircraft as they are evacuated by US military personnel during Operation Urgent Fury.

Reagan pronounced the mission a great victory over the tiny nation, but international reaction was overwhelmingly negative. The United Nations General Assembly condemned it as "a flagrant violation of international law." Nevertheless, the date of the invasion is now a national holiday in Grenada called Thanksgiving Day.

the US president, justified the invasion by citing the threat to the approximately one thousand Americans who were on the island at the time. Many of them were medical students at Grenada's medical school.

In the fighting, nineteen Americans and more than sixty Grenadian and Cuban troops were killed. Many more were injured. The Americans quickly installed an interim government and restored the island's constitution. Elections were held in December 1985.

After dropping off American troops to participate in Operation Urgent Fury, US Army UH-60 Black Hawk helicopters depart Point Salines Airfield in Grenada.

STABILITY

In 1986, seventeen people were tried for their connection to the assassination of Maurice Bishop, including the coup's mastermind, Bernard Coard. Most of the so-called Grenada Seventeen were found guilty and received death sentences, but those were eventually commuted. Most of the convicts insisted they were not involved in the murders. By 2009, all of the men were released from prison after serving lighter sentences. Internationally, some observers questioned the integrity of the trials, with Amnesty International reporting in 2003 that the arrests and trial had been a miscarriage of justice. In 2009, Grenada's international airport in Saint George's was renamed Maurice Bishop International Airport in honor of the late prime minister.

In recent decades, Grenada has enjoyed relative stability. In 2013, Keith Mitchell (b. 1946) of the New National Party became prime minister, after having served previously in that post from 1995 to 2008. As of 2019, he remains the country's prime minister.

Other events of note have included money laundering allegations against the country's banking industry in the early 2000s and two destructive hurricanes. In 2004, Hurricane Ivan damaged 90 percent of the island's buildings and killed thirty-nine people. The following year, while the island was still trying to recover from Ivan's devastation, Hurricane Emily caused further damage and killed one person.

INTERNET LINKS

https://www.bbc.com/news/world-latin-america-19596901
This BBC timeline presents a chronology of key events in Grenada's history.

https://www.blackpast.org/global-african-history/bishop -maurice-1944-1983
A brief biography of Maurice Bishop is offered on this site.

https://www.britannica.com/place/Grenada
The online encyclopedia offers an up-to-date overview of the island's history.

https://www.caribbeanlifenews.com/stories/2015/6/2015-05-29 -nk-marryshow-cl.html
An article about Theophilus A. Marryshow is presented on this site.

https://www.globalpolicy.org/component/content/article/ 155/25966.html
This site offers an in-depth examination of the US invasion of Grenada.

https://www.gov.gd/biographies/keith_mitchell_bio.html
The Grenada government site includes a biography of Prime Minister Keith Mitchell.

https://www.independent.co.uk/news/people/obituary-sir-eric -gairy-1247273.html
Eric M. Gairy's obituary in the *Independent* portrays the former leader's rise and fall.

https://www.nytimes.com/1983/10/20/world/leader-of-grenada-is -reported-killed-by-troops.html
This archival article reports on the assassination of Maurice Bishop.

HOUSES OF PARLIAMENT

GOVERNMENT

Queen Elizabeth II stands at the Houses of Parliament, York House, in Saint George's on October 31, 1985.

3

QUEEN ELIZABETH II OF THE UNITED Kingdom is the queen of Grenada. This is because Grenada is a constitutional monarchy and a member of the Commonwealth. The Queen—or the reigning British monarch—functions as the head of state. She is represented in Grenada by a governor-general, who acts on her behalf. This status is largely ceremonial but not unimportant.

In reality, Grenada is ruled by its elected government officials, a bicameral (two-house) parliament consisting of a fifteen-member House of Representatives and a thirteen-member Senate. The prime minister is the head of government and is the leader of the party that wins the majority of seats in elections. All Grenadians over eighteen years of age are eligible to vote, and there are multiple political parties.

All of this is spelled out in the country's constitution, which was adopted in 1973 and which came into force in 1974 when the country became an independent state within the Commonwealth.

THE CONSTITUTION

Written and adopted when the country became an independent nation, the Grenadian constitution spells out the rights, freedoms, and responsibilities

The flag of Grenada is divided diagonally into two yellow triangles (top and bottom) and two green triangles, with a red border on all sides. Three yellow stars in the top red border and another three on the bottom stand for the nation's six parishes. A larger star in the center is for the capital, Saint George's. A symbolic nutmeg pod appears to the side. Yellow represents the sun and the warmth of the people, green stands for vegetation and agriculture, and red symbolizes courage.

Grenada is a Commonwealth realm. As such, it is an independent country unto itself and yet it is also part of the British monarchy. How can this be?

The Commonwealth of Nations, usually called simply the Commonwealth, is a political association of sovereign nations that are former territories of the British Empire. The members are united by their common history and heritage, the English language, and a democratic culture that values the rule of constitutional law and human rights. The Commonwealth operated without a charter until 2013, when it formalized its values in sixteen core beliefs: democracy; human rights; international peace and security; tolerance, respect, and understanding; freedom of expression; separation of powers; the rule of law; good governance; sustainable development; protecting the environment; access to health, education, food, and shelter; gender equality; the importance of young people in the Commonwealth; recognition of the needs of small states; recognition of the needs of vulnerable states; and the role of civil society.

There are fifty-three member countries in the Commonwealth, and membership is

Grenada's 1977 postage stamp commemorates the twenty-fifth anniversary of the coronation of Queen Elizabeth II.

voluntary. A member that does not abide by Commonwealth values can be suspended, as happened to Nigeria in 1995 and Fiji in 2009. This may occur when a democratic government is overthrown in a coup, typically by an authoritarian regime that abolishes constitutional democracy.

Of the fifty-three members, only sixteen are realms. These members, including Grenada, recognize the Queen as their monarch. Thirty-one member nations are republics, and the remaining five—all in Africa or Southeast Asia—recognize other monarchs or royal houses.

of the citizens. The Grenadian people enjoy a wide range of civil and political rights guaranteed by the constitution, including freedom of speech, press, worship, and association. They have a right to life, personal liberty, privacy, and a fair trial. They have the right not be subjected to slavery or forced labor, and the right not to be discriminated against. The constitution gives citizens the right to change their government peacefully through democratic elections. The duties of citizenship are relatively few and include the responsibility to follow the law; to participate in the economic, political, and social life of the state in a manner that advances national unity; and to protect, preserve, and improve the environment.

RECENT ELECTIONS

The prime minister is the head of government. Since 2013, that position has been filled by

Keith Mitchell, prime minister of Grenada, speaks at the 2005 World Summit for the sixtieth session of the United Nations General Assembly in New York.

Keith Mitchell of the New National Party (NNP), a moderate conservative party. Mitchell has served as prime minister before, from 1995 to 2008.

In the 2008 elections, the National Democratic Congress (NDC), a moderate liberal party, won the most seats, and the prime minister position went to Tillman Thomas (b. 1947).

However, in subsequent elections in 2013, the NNP not only won the majority, but also swept all fifteen parliamentary seats. Mitchell returned as prime minister. In 2018, the victory was duplicated as the NNP retained all fifteen seats, making it the second time in Grenadian history that a political party swept the election. It also brought Mitchell back yet again for another term. At this writing, he is the longest-serving prime minister in Grenada's history.

ECONOMY

British tourists view cocoa beans being dried in the open air at the Belmont Estate in Belmont, Grenada. The estate was first established in the 1600s.

4

A FTER HURRICANE IVAN HIT Grenada in 2004, Grenada was a wasteland. In addition to the human toll—with thirty-nine deaths, about seven hundred injuries, and eighteen thousand left homeless—the catastrophe turned the country's economy completely upside down. The previously growing economy plunged into decline. Some 90 percent of Grenada's buildings were damaged or destroyed, including almost every school. Tourism was brought to an abrupt halt. Some 80 percent of the nutmeg trees were blown down, as well as most of the island's forest cover.

Then, just as the island nation was beginning to recover, the global financial crisis of 2008—2009 happened, significantly slowing investment and other economic opportunities for the country, which was already deeply in debt.

In 2018, Grenada reached a historic milestone, with more than five hundred thousand tourists visiting the country. Tourism plays a crucial role in the nation's economy, and the increase in visitors aligns with the economy's growth in general over recent years.

A fisherman carries supplies on the dock at Carenage Harbor in Saint George's.

to June bring in tuna, kingfish, flying fish, and dolphin fish. This accounts for about half of the year's catch. For the rest of the year, fishermen have a good time harvesting bottom-dwelling snapper, grouper, and other tropical rockfish. Another kind of fishing involves catching shellfish, including lobsters and conchs, and turtles. White sea urchins are harvested for their eggs. The eggs are collected and put into clean sea urchin cases, then baked and sold.

The fishing industry has received a lot of foreign aid, particularly from Venezuela and Japan. This has made possible the construction of fish centers where the catch can be stored in cold rooms. Most of the catch from Carriacou and Petite Martinique is sold to exporters. There are public fish markets in Grenada, but fishermen still sell their fish directly from their landing site.

TOURISM

In 2018, more than a half million tourists—528,077 visitors—came to Grenada, a record high number and a 12.9 percent increase over the previous year. Most of Grenada's tourists are day-trippers who arrive by cruise ships that dock at the pier in Saint George's harbor, one of the most beautiful deep-water harbors in the Caribbean. When passengers disembark, they find that they are immediately in the heart of the capital city, with all major attractions just a short distance away. A nearby vendors' market becomes a hive of activity on cruise-ship days, with stalls set up to sell food, clothing, and souvenirs.

Grenada's busy international airport brings thousands more tourists by air each year. More than fifty establishments, ranging from small budget guesthouses to luxurious hotels with hundreds of rooms, provide accommodations. In 2018, about 160,970 tourists stayed more than one day, an increase of almost 10 percent in that category. An increase in tourists

The *Royal Princess* cruise ship pulls into harbor carrying more than three thousand visitors to Saint George's.

brings more business to hotels and restaurants, along with support services and small vendors.

In addition to the magnificent beaches, more and more people are coming for the Spicemas festivities in August, programs at Saint George's University, and such regional and international events as the Grenada Invitational Athletics Meet, Dive Fest, and Pure Grenada Music Festival. Ecotourism is also a growing trend.

SMALL INDUSTRIES

The construction sector has been good, helped by major building projects at Saint George's University, Silver Sands Resort, and the Parliament Building.

Manufacturing makes up a small portion of the country's GDP. The older industries are garment and furniture making, food and fruit preserving and canning, rum distillation, and cottage industries such as jewelry making and woodworking. These are still important in the country, but newer industries such as industrial gases, paints and varnishes, and flour and animal feeds are being encouraged. In recent years, the government has diversified the economy with the development of a manufacturing sector focused on paper products and electronic components, offshore financial services, and direct marketing.

Besides nutmeg, cocoa, mace, bananas, and other fruit, Grenada's principal exports include chocolate, vegetables, fish, and clothing. Imports include food and beverages, fuel and lubricants, machinery, transportation equipment, and other manufactured goods.

Grenada's main trading partners are the other members of the Organization of Eastern Caribbean States (OECS), particularly Saint Vincent, Dominica, Saint Lucia, and Antigua; members of the Caribbean Community (CARICOM), such as Jamaica, Guyana, Barbados, Bahamas, and Trinidad; other Caribbean states; the European Union; the United States; Japan; and China.

OVER LAND AND SEA

The Maurice Bishop International Airport at Point Salines in the south of the island is Grenada's connection with the rest of the world. It is linked by air to other Caribbean states by LIAT (Leeward Islands Air Transport), the region's main air carrier, which is headquartered in Antigua. Several other smaller airline companies also operate inter-island routes. SVG Air, the airline of Saint Vincent and the Grenadines, connects the islands with the main island of Grenada. There is a small airport at Lauriston on Carriacou.

On the sea, ferries and shipping lines operate trips regularly between the many harbors of Grenada, Carriacou, and Petite Martinique, and between Grenada and the other Caribbean islands.

The Grenadian transportation network is well developed, and most of the roads, including those on Carriacou and Petite Martinique, are paved, although extremely narrow, winding, and steep. The main road on Grenada circles the island, linking Saint George's with all the coastal villages.

Cars drive carefully through the Sendall Tunnel in Saint George's. The narrow tunnel was built in 1894 for horse-drawn carriages.

INTERNET LINKS

https://www.cia.gov/library/publications/the-world-factbook/geos/gj.html

The *CIA World Factbook* provides up-to-date statistics about Grenada's economy.

https://www.undp.org/content/undp/en/home/blog/2017/3/1/From-Spice-Isle-to-Blue-Innovation-hub-Grenada-s-vision-for-the-future.html

This article explains Grenada's plan for building a blue economy.

ENVIRONMENT

A Grenada mona monkey (*Cercopithecus mona*) sits among the lush foliage of a tree.

5

MUCH OF GRENADA IS MADE UP OF land that has been cultivated or altered from its natural state in some way. Nonindigenous plants and animals have been introduced and flourished, often to the detriment of the native species. Intensive use of Grenada's natural resources plus poor agricultural practices, overfishing, industrialization, and urbanization have had negative effects.

However, there is now a greater awareness of the problems. Like people in many other parts of the world, Grenadians realize that they have to care for their environment, and policies have been put in place to make sure that the country's natural resources are used wisely. Grenada is also climatically vulnerable. It is located within the hurricane belt and periodically suffers tremendous damage from these wild tropical storms. Furthermore, the global climate change crisis, with its threat of rising sea levels, will have a particular impact upon this island nation.

USING THE LAND WISELY

Agriculture is considered an important socioeconomic activity for Grenadians. The "Isle of Spice" produces nutmeg and other spices, such as cinnamon, clove, and bay leaf. It is famous for its bananas and cocoa.

Of the 182 countries in the Climate Risk Index, which evaluated climate-related losses during the period between 1997 and 2017, Grenada was in the top 2 percent for losses due to climate-related natural disasters and in the top 5 percent of climate disaster fatalities.

The spectacled caiman (*Caiman crocodilus*), also known as the white caiman or common caiman, is a crocodilian reptile found in Grenada.

The government is working to improve management of these areas to ensure that the demands of agricultural use and the need for fresh water are balanced. The national parks are a refuge for Grenada's many species of birds, mammals, and reptiles, especially those that are now rare, threatened, and endangered through loss of habitat and excessive hunting. Among the endangered species are the Grenada hook-billed kite, the tundra peregrine falcon, the green and hawksbill sea turtles, the spectacled caiman, and the Orinoco crocodile.

The Grand Etang Forest is the habitat of the rare nine-banded armadillo. This mammal, known locally as the tatu, is a game animal and can sometimes end up on the kitchen table as food. There are two species of opossum in Grenada: the Robinson's mouse opossum and the large opossum. Both are considered rare. Like the armadillo, the large opossum is hunted for its meat.

FRESHWATER SUPPLY
AND THE OCEAN

Grenada has limited freshwater supplies. The water is in great demand for domestic, agricultural, and industrial use. The country is small and mountainous. Its climate is humid and tropical, and instead of dividing the year into spring, summer, fall, and winter, people divide it into wet and dry seasons. The dry season runs from January to May, and the wet season from June to December. This rain feeds the rivers, streams, lakes, and ponds that are the main sources of fresh water. However, unless there are storage facilities in which the rainwater can be stored until needed, most of this supply flows down the steep slopes and into the sea.

A beautiful sand beach in Grenada is marred by the accumulation of trash.

There are a few watershed areas—Annandale, Concord, and Mount Hope and Clabony. These are protected areas. There is also some groundwater in the northwest part of Grenada Island. Environmental concerns relating to the supply of fresh water have to do with the quality as well as the quantity. The increasing demand from farmers for agricultural land has caused many of them to enter the diminishing forested areas and clear the land for planting. This has caused deforestation of the island and soil erosion, as the cleared land allows for greater water runoff to occur, resulting in the fertile topsoil being washed into rivers and streams and carried into the ocean. In addition, opening up more land for human use creates more pollution of the streams and the rivers. This further reduces the amount of fresh water available.

Pollution of the coastal waters is another environmental issue that the government of Grenada has been concerned about. The coastal waters and reefs are polluted with solid waste and other debris. Annual cleanups of the reefs and beaches turn up a lot of junk such as plastic bottles and food containers. Cruise and commercial ships that use Grenada's sea lanes and dock in its ports have to be careful of how they get rid of their solid wastes. They are required to dispose of their waste in an environmentally careful manner, but monitoring this has not been easy.

Another large and ultraluxurious resort in the south of the island, on Grand Anse Beach, presents itself as being environmentally conscious. Among other green initiatives, it does not use chlorine in its swimming pools (chlorine is harmful to the environment). It buys food that is grown locally and organically, composts its kitchen and garden wastes, has its own vegetable and herb garden, uses solar energy, and makes its own fresh water with a desalination plant that removes salt from seawater.

Sailing is another important activity in Grenada that impacts the environment. Many local residents are keen sailors, and the island's tropical waters and deep and sheltered harbors attract sailors from all over the world. The development of mooring facilities and marinas contributes much to the economy of the country and to the lifestyle of the people.

Through legislation and education, the government is making sure that those involved in developing and maintaining marinas where motorboats and sailboats can be docked take steps to protect the environment. This includes

The Workboat Regatta is a popular sailing festival that takes place annually off Grand Anse Beach.

cleaning up the lagoons where marinas are located, installing docks that have as little impact on the environment as possible, monitoring the dumping of wastes, and ensuring that boat repairs do not cause toxic chemicals to enter and pollute the waters. Increasingly, special mooring facilities are being built and improved so that boats in the lagoons are able to tie onto them, thus removing the need to drop their anchors onto the seabed, an action that damages the marine environment.

A tourist diving party prepares to take off from Grand Anse Beach.

PRESERVING THE CORAL REEFS

Grenada has an extensive network of coral reefs. Scuba diving is an important segment of the tourism industry, and there are numerous dive sites just off the shores of the islands. Carriacou is Arawak for "island of reefs." Again, tourism is an important factor in the health of these reefs, and its impact can be both good and bad for this environment. The reefs are very fragile, and while they take a very long time to grow, they can be damaged in an instant by a carelessly dropped anchor or chain from a boat or even by a diver who comes into contact with them.

There is growing awareness among Grenadians that it is important to preserve this habitat not just because it is a big money earner for the country but also because our environment has to be cared for and not depleted through carelessness and greed. Grenada's reef environment is protected, and it is illegal to remove any corals, sponges, or other reef life from these waters. A sporting and fishing license is required for fishing in the waters.

The Grenada Scuba Diving Association organizes regular cleanups of dive areas, marine parks, and beaches. Commonly found items are plastic food containers and cups, bottles, and discarded fishing lines.

CLIMATE CHANGE

In 2019, Grenadian prime minister Keith Mitchell called climate change an "existential threat" for the people of the Caribbean islands. "We see the plight of our farmers with respect to changes in rainfall patterns … We know the bountiful shoals of fish that have historically fed us are being decimated by warming waters and acidifying oceans. We see our disappearing coastal landscapes and ecosystems. We are experiencing the devastating economic and social impacts," he said. He further decried inaction on the part of larger, more powerful nations.

The issue of climate change—and the global warming connected to it—does indeed have great significance for Grenada. One major concern is the rising sea levels brought about by melting glaciers in Earth's polar regions. The Intergovernmental Panel on Climate Change (IPCC), made up of scientists from around the world, has estimated that in the past century sea levels rose by 7 inches (17 cm) because of the increase in Earth's temperature. Further rises in sea levels can be expected, and it has been predicted that by the end of this century the sea level could rise by 7 to 23 inches (18 to 59 cm). This would cause the loss of a significant portion of Grenada's coastline through flooding and destroy the mangrove forests, the harbor, and much of the livable space.

In addition, scientists have said that increased levels of the greenhouse gas carbon dioxide in the atmosphere are affecting the coral reefs in two ways—through the rise in the temperature of the water and through an increase in its acidity. Increased environmental stress causes the corals to be bleached (lose their color) and become weaker and more prone to disease. When carbon dioxide dissolves in seawater, making it more acidic, it affects the way in which the coral reef is formed. Reefs are made up of calcium carbonate, produced by tiny creatures called coral polyps. Researchers have found that the increased acidity of the water slows the polyps' production of calcium carbonate.

Some studies have also shown that reef-forming coral cannot survive in water that is too acidic. As the reefs are a habitat for many species of fish and other marine life, the dying of the coral would affect the entire ecosystem of the reef. The destruction of this ecosystem, besides removing a beautiful natural environment, would have dire effects on the economy of the country, affecting the fishing and tourism industries and the people as a whole.

A third blow that climate change will deliver to the small nation of Grenada is in the area of hurricanes. There has been evidence since the 1970s that a correlation exists between the number of intense tropical storms and increases in the temperature of the sea. It is very likely that the increase in greenhouse gases has contributed to the rise in the sea surface temperatures in regions of hurricane formation.

As a very small country, Grenada can do little to fight global warming and climate change. As part of the Caribbean community of nations, however, it has joined its neighbors in planning for the effects of climate change. This has included monitoring and analyzing climate and sea-level trends, identifying areas that are particularly vulnerable, and developing a management plan for an effective response to the impact of climate change. In addition, the government is participating in United Nations environmental efforts and negotiations such as the Paris Climate Agreement and has begun imposing environmental levies on cruise-ship passengers to fund efforts to reduce beach erosion and control tourism-related pollution. Grenada is also a party to many other international environmental treaties, including those on biodiversity, endangered species, whaling, and ozone protection.

INTERNET LINKS

https://www.cnn.com/2019/05/21/opinions/caribbean-climate -change-leaders-grenada-prime-minister-mitchell/index.html
This article about the climate change emergency was authored by Keith Mitchell, the prime minister of Grenada.

http://www.iccas.gd
This is the site concerned with Grenada's plans to adapt to climate change.

GRENADIANS

A woman carries cocoa pods on her head.

6

GRENADIANS ARE OFTEN SAID TO BE the friendliest people on earth— at least according to numerous tourism sites. Many other countries make the same boast, but this positive attribute of Grenada's people seems to be generally accurate. Most of the island's people, while certainly not wealthy, live reasonably happy lives, enriched by their natural setting, a relatively stable government, abundant food, and an upbeat traditional culture.

More than 80 percent of all Grenadians are of African descent, while the remainder of the population consists of small percentages of East Indians, Europeans, and others. However, to assume that Grenadians are only African in ethnicity is too narrow a view. Many have English, French, Dutch, Portuguese, Polish, Amerindian, or Chinese ancestors as well.

When the Spanish first arrived in the Caribbean, they found three major groups of indigenous people. The Ciboneys lived on the northwestern tip of Cuba and Hispaniola. The Bahamas, Greater Antilles, and Trinidad were dominated by the Arawaks, while the Caribs were found on the Virgin Islands, many islands of the Lesser Antilles, and the northwestern tip of Trinidad.

The wealthiest people in Grenada (and other Caribbean nations) are disproportionately resident foreigners. The Grenadian government actively recruits such foreigners, offering citizenship in return for investment. However, the influx of money to the cash-strapped island is potentially offset by the possibility of illicit or illegal financial activity.

LIFESTYLE

The village of Bura is nestled in the
mountainous center of Grenada.

7

THANKS TO BALMY TROPICAL WINDS, warm temperatures, and a relaxed attitude, life on Grenada moves at a slower pace than in the United States. Visitors to the island quickly adapt to this leisurely pace, and much has been said about the Caribbean islanders' lack of a sense of urgency.

Villages are strung out along the main island highway, houses clinging to the hillsides and congregating where there is sufficient space to form little communities. Each village has at least one church, a school or two, the village green where local soccer matches are played, and numerous corner drink and grocery shops.

The church is an important anchor in Grenadian life. All life events—a birth in the family, marriage, and death—are celebrated there. As in many other parts of the world, however, the old traditions have less influence on people today.

VILLAGE RHYTHMS

Grenada's villages are mainly fishing and farming communities where life is not ruled by the clock. Fishermen put their boats out in the morning and come back at the end of the day with their catch. They blow on a conch shell to announce that they have fish to sell. When a fishing boat comes in, everyone, especially the children, goes down to the beach, curious to see what the catch is.

Grenada is considered one of the safest of the Caribbean islands in terms of crime. In 2017, the murder rate was 9 per 100,000 citizens. This was far lower than the rate of 56 per 100,000 in Saint Kitts and Nevis, or 36 per 100,000 in Saint Vincent and the Grenadines for the same period. Nevertheless, Grenada scores considerably higher in sexual assaults, burglaries, and drug-related crimes.

Colorfully painted houses in Grenada glow with a happy Caribbean vibe.

Houses are usually simple and rectangular in shape, with two or three bedrooms, a living area, a kitchen, and a bathroom. If more space is required, a wooden shed may be added to the side. Bushes with colorful leaves and flowers are often planted in the front and serve to divide one yard from another. Vegetable gardens flourish behind the houses together with many fruit trees. A family may own some chickens along with a few goats and cows tethered to a nearby tree or post. If they have a small plot of land to farm, whole families will be engaged in agriculture.

MARKET DAY

Markets are integral to a Grenadian's life. Women cultivate vegetables for their families and take the excess to the market to sell. The market functions most of the week except Sunday, from early morning to late afternoon. It is most lively on Saturdays. The largest Saturday markets are in the towns of Saint George's and Grenville.

Stalls are often nothing more than makeshift boxes of scrap wood nailed together, topped off with large and colorful umbrellas. People gather not only to shop for the items they need but also to spend time chatting with their friends. The streets are filled with groups of men and women "liming," as a Grenadian might say, meaning just standing around and relaxing with friends.

People enjoy walking past outdoor vendors in Saint George's.

Meat and fish are sold at specialized markets such as the Melville Street Fish Market and Abattoir on Grenada Island. Women sell mainly small fish called jacks from wooden trays set upon pails full of fish. A carved-up green turtle is occasionally part of the morning's offering. Every Friday night, stalls sprout on the streets of Gouyave. The vendors cook local fish delicacies in a food fair called the Gouyave Fish Festival.

TRANSPORTATION

The family car is often a small sedan, but pickups and four-wheel drive vehicles are fairly common. Bicycles and motorbikes are commonly seen on weekends, when young boys whiz down the streets on their way to the beach. Those without their own means of transportation walk wherever they can. For longer journeys, a taxi or a bus is indispensable.

Taxis are costly and are preferred by tourists. Most Grenadians use buses, which are actually minivans that carry up to eighteen passengers comfortably.

The bus is operated by a driver and his assistant, who try to get as many people in the bus as they can to maximize the revenue from each trip. Buses crammed with passengers are a common sight. As Grenada's roads are narrow and winding, a bus ride can often be a hair-raising experience.

Bus terminals are in the heart of Saint George's near Market Square and the Esplanade, and bus routes fan out from there to cover the entire island. Although there are bus stops, buses will pick up passengers anywhere along the route, even though it is illegal to do so.

GRENADIAN WOMEN

Women have always been a source of cheap unskilled and semiskilled labor in Grenada. During the days of slavery, they were field and house slaves. After emancipation, they became laborers on plantations. They later worked in factories. If they did not have a job outside the home, they planted gardens and sold their extra provisions in the market to earn money.

Women are still employed in traditionally female occupations today. Many of them are in domestic service or work as seamstresses, hairdressers, and factory workers. The more educated are often teachers and nurses, or they work in the service sector, such as in tourism. A small number hold administrative and senior management positions in private companies, public service, and political office.

Grenadian women have always had the major responsibility for caring for and nurturing the family, even when the male head of the household is present. Many have to work outside the home to supplement the family income. Having their own money gives them a sense of independence, self-esteem, and power in their family and community.

The Grenadian government set up Cedars Shelter for abused women and children in 1999. This center provides temporary shelter and counseling for women and children in need of help.

Small colorful minibuses are the most popular form of local public transportation.

THE FAMILY UNIT

Grenadians tend to be traditional and conservative in their outlook. The family unit is important, and the concept of family goes beyond immediate members to embrace extended members, close friends, and neighbors. That said, however, single-parent families—headed mostly by women—are quite common.

Most women are expected to bear children and to be responsible for their care and upbringing. Women tend to bear children at an early age. In the late 1990s, the average Grenadian woman gave birth to three or four children, but the fertility rate has dropped since then to two children in 2019. Teenage pregnancies are common and often result in the young women having to leave school prematurely. Women who have no children of their own often care for the children of others. Therefore, besides their mothers, children may be raised by other close relatives, family friends, or neighbors.

In return, the children are expected to look after their parents in their old age. Parents look forward to their children doing well and being able to financially support them. Respect for elders and sharing among the family are instilled in children when they are very young.

Families congregate outside a school building, waiting for the school day to begin.

education. School dropout rates are among the lowest in the Caribbean, with more boys than girls leaving school before graduation.

Secondary school lasts five years, during which students prepare for an examination set by the Caribbean Examination Council, after which they may move on to a pre-university level of studies at the Grenada National College. Only about 20 percent achieve this level of education.

Except for a few private ones, schools are coeducational. Young Grenadians can also choose to attend technical and vocational institutes to study agriculture, secretarial skills, drafting, auto mechanics, plumbing, and other courses. Saint George's University is the highest institution of learning in Grenada. It began as a school of medicine in 1977 but has since expanded to include arts and sciences and a school of graduate studies. Students can also attend a branch of the University of the West Indies in Grenada.

RITUALS OF DEATH

The rituals that accompany a death incorporate both Christian practices and folk beliefs. The family of the deceased is responsible for the funeral preparations. During the wake, the men and boys will build the coffin in one corner of the yard, while the women and girls prepare mourning clothes, head cloths, and ribbons for the mourners. Food and drinks are prepared—usually tea or coffee with bread or biscuits and rum. A spicy tea made from the leaves of a native bush was traditionally served, but coffee is a modern substitute.

On the day of the burial, the coffin is taken to church or the cemetery. Hymns are sung along the way. Two chairs are taken along on which to place the coffin if a change of pallbearers is required. At the entrance to the cemetery, the chairs are turned upside down to allow the spirit of the dead to leave the chairs. When the bearers are relieved of their burden, they shake out their arms to transfer the spirit back to the coffin. An evergreen tree is planted to mark the tomb. Relatives who visit after the funeral throw water and rum on it. A prayer meeting is also held after the funeral at the house where the death occurred. On that day, a *saraca* (SAH-ra-ka), or special sacrificial feast, is prepared. A tombstone for the grave is not erected until enough time has passed to allow the earth to settle.

The placing of the stone requires a stone feast. The stone is first placed on the main bed in the house, and a sacrificial plate of food is placed on a table. The stone is then taken outside where it is blessed with a sprinkling of water, rum, rice, and eggs. Prayers are said before it is ceremoniously taken to the cemetery and placed on the grave. Then, a Big Drum ceremony is held, followed by much feasting and dancing. The food is cooked in big pots and includes stewed peas, ground provisions (root vegetables), bananas, rolled rice, coo-coo (ground cornmeal cooked into a cake with coconut, salt, and water), and plenty of meat—pork, chicken, and mutton.

INTERNET LINKS

https://www.osac.gov/Content/Report/361e3bc6-3324-44e9-b921 -15f4ae5e3230
The US State Department Overseas Security Advisory Council 2018 report on crime and safety in Barbados and Grenada is available on this site.

https://www.unicef.org/easterncaribbean/ECA_GRENADA_SitAn_ Web.pdf
This UNICEF report takes an in-depth look at the state of children's well-being in Grenada.

RELIGION

Christ of the Deep, a statue that stands looking out to sea on the coast of Saint George's, commemorates the *Bianca C*, a ship that burned and sank in 1961.

8

GRENADA IS A PREDOMINANTLY Christian nation. About half the people are Protestants—mostly Pentecostals or Seventh Day Adventists—and another 36 percent are Roman Catholics. This dominance of Christianity is a direct result of European colonization.

When the Europeans first arrived in the Caribbean centuries ago, they thought that the indigenous people they encountered—the Arawaks and Caribs—had no religion. Although these people did not have a religion recognizable to the Europeans, they did have beliefs that were of a religious or supernatural nature.

The indigenous people were animists, believing in the existence of many spirits that could influence human life. These spirits were associated with natural elements or phenomena that they controlled. They could inhabit physical objects, which the natives worshipped, and people could be possessed by spirits. When this happened, the spirit had to be exorcized by a priest or shaman.

These people had a clear sense of what it meant to be good or bad. For the Caribs, it was good to be courageous and resourceful in battle, as they were a warlike people. Good behavior for the Arawaks, on the other hand, was to be gentle and peace-loving.

The Europeans tried to convert the indigenous people to the Christian faith. Throughout much of the Greater Antilles, the conquering and "civilizing" was done by the Spanish. However, on Grenada, as on many other islands of the Lesser Antilles, the task was undertaken by the French. In the process, hostilities between the French colonizers and the Caribs

broke out, leading to the expulsion and extermination of all Carib people on the island of Grenada.

ARRIVAL OF THE DOMINICANS

With the French colonial government came the establishment of the Roman Catholic religion. The first Roman Catholic missionary group to arrive in Grenada was the Dominican order. The Dominicans were given land to help establish them in their missionary work. They were followed by the Capuchins, who in 1690 built a church in Fort Royal, then another one in the capital. An Anglican church now stands on that site.

When Grenada was ceded to the British in 1763, the British government established the Church of England (or the Anglican Church) on the island. This led to the persecution of the Roman Catholic Church until 1795. Roman

Catholic relics, altars, and baptismal fonts were destroyed. The settlers on Grenada, who were mainly French, were pressured to give up their Roman Catholic faith and embrace Anglicanism. Many fled to Trinidad to escape the persecution, taking their slaves with them.

Church members join hands during a baptism ceremony.

MAIN CHRISTIAN CHURCHES

By the 1800s, four main Christian denominations were active in Grenada: the Anglicans, the Roman Catholics, the Methodists, and the Presbyterians, or the Church of Scotland. These churches competed for converts. The Anglican Church had the support of the colonial government and was a rich landowner. Along with the Church of Scotland, it attracted the ruling class and the planters. The Roman Catholic Church had the greatest number of working-class followers.

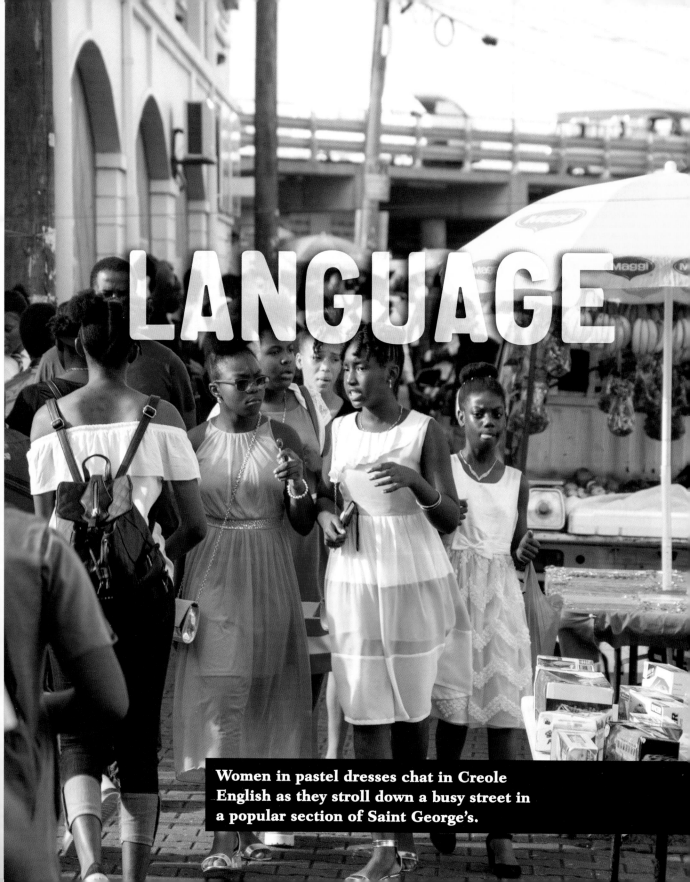

LANGUAGE

Women in pastel dresses chat in Creole English as they stroll down a busy street in a popular section of Saint George's.

9

ENGLISH IS THE LANGUAGE OF Grenada—the official language used in the government, courts, and schools. Throughout the island nation, however, what is heard is English with a distinctive Caribbean lilt.

When enslaved people were first brought from Africa to work on the plantations, they brought with them their own various languages, but laborers, overseers, and plantation owners all had to learn to communicate with each other. This was achieved through a natural process called the creolization of a language.

When Grenada was a French colony, the people spoke a creole that was a mixture of French and African dialects. When the British took control of the country, Grenadians changed to a creole based on English. Today, the old French creole, which the Grenadians call Patois (pat-WAH), is almost extinct, spoken only by a few older people.

CREOLE ENGLISH

There was a tendency in the past for people of the upper classes to speak Standard English and for those of the lower classes to speak a creolized dialect. This has resulted in a lingering "colonial" attitude toward language. It was a badge of good breeding and social class to speak "the Queen's English" or "BBC English" (that spoken by a British Broadcasting Corporation announcer), and to acquire a refined English accent was highly desirable.

SOME COMMON CREOLE EXPRESSIONS

Just now	*Don't expect something immediately*
Now for now.	*Right away*
Don't make me vex	*Don't make me angry*
Don't mamaguy me.	*Don't tell me a lie*
Comess.	*A total confusion*
Fete.	*A party*
For so.	*For no reason*
Fete for so	*A party on the spur of the moment*
Like bush, like peas	*There is a lot of whatever it is*
Fete as bush	*A grand party with plenty to eat and drink*
Brango	*Spicy gossip*
Play lougarou	*Play the fool*
Sea bath	*A swim*
Lime	*Relax, hang around*
Beating mouth.	*Chatting*
Farse	*Nosey*
Fire one	*Drink rum*
Me tell you.	*I'm telling you*
You too sut.	*You are too stupid*
Make a blow.	*Buy a drink*
Study your head.	*Be careful what you say or do*
Pork ah pork no beef	*Not of the best*
Don't give me a six for nine	*Don't mislead me*
The firm big	*The family has money*
Watch your case.	*Be careful*
Wood have ears	*Someone may be listening*

Grenadian educator and author Clyde Belfon, who has made a study of the language of his people, believes that Creole English rather than Standard English (the English that Grenadians learn in school) is the first language of the people. It has its own syntax, vocabulary, rhythm, and meaning. There

is, however, a stigma associated with Creole English—many believe that it is "bad English," the language of uneducated people.

Linguists would disagree, however. Though a creole develops through the mixture of different languages, it becomes a unique language unto itself and serves as the mother tongue for the people who speak it.

A welcome sign in English promotes Grenada's "spicy" reputation.

THE FRENCH CONNECTION

Language keeps history alive. Many place names in Grenada are French, reflecting the French colonial era centuries back. These include such names as Gouyave ("Guava"), Grand Etang ("Great Lake"), and Lance aux Epines (from L'Anse aux Epines, or "Beach of Pines"). Many words in today's Grenadian Creole come from French and Creole French. The first day of Carnival, for example, is called J'ouvert (jou-vay) from *jour ouvert*, meaning "the beginning of day." Lajabless, the she-devil that storytellers frighten little children with, comes from *la diablesse*, meaning "female devil." There are also expressions derived from French. "Well yes, oui!" is often used to express exasperation

ARTS

A local artist paints a vivid image at the Grand Anse Craft and Spice Market.

10

The Spicemas festival of Carnival in August is a joyful celebration of Grenadian arts and culture, expressed in music, dance, and vivid costumes.

THE ARTS OF GRENADA SHARE A great deal with Caribbean arts in general. The music, in particular, has a distinctive Caribbean flavor. Whether calypso, reggae, or soca, music can be heard everywhere—on the streets, in the buses or taxis, on the beach, or wherever there are people. Much of the music has its roots in African folk music, with drumming and strong rhythms.

Where there is music, there must be dance! Grenadian culture is vibrant with both, inspired by African traditions along with European and American influences.

The arts scene is thriving, with folk artists, craftspeople, and storytellers. The modern version of the storyteller is found in the theater and in the oral poetry performed in front of large crowds. Even the houses on the island are a canvas for artistic expression. Their colorful exteriors display the exuberance and joy of Grenadian creativity.

CALYPSO AND SOCA

Calypso music had its beginnings in Trinidad in the eighteenth century, and from there it spread to the rest of the region. Calypso came about when slaves working on the plantations started to sing satirical songs in French Patois. It was their way of mocking their European masters and expressing their discontent. Sometimes singers would try to outdo each other in a battle of words and verbal insults. The lyrics of early calypso songs were often composed on the spot, showing the creativity and wit of the singers.

Today, calypso is usually sung in English. The songs are still satirical and biting in their commentary on social and political conditions, exposing sham, pretense, and injustice on the Grenadian islands. The melody and the rhythms are similar, but the lyrics change from song to song.

Calypso competitions are an important part of the Carnival celebrations, when many singers vie for the title of Calypso King. The singers like to take on special expressive names such as Attila the Hun, King Pharaoh, Lord Executor, and Duke of Iron.

Soca music, which stands for "soul of calypso," also came out of Trinidad. Invented in 1970 by the musician Lord Shorty, it's a sped up form of calypso with an Indian twist. Soca has evolved into a younger, more energetic form

Musicians perform outside the Forest Reserve Visitor Center at Grand Etang National Park.

One famous calypso singer is Slinger Francisco, better known as the Mighty Sparrow, or simply Sparrow (shown here). Born in Grenada in 1935, Sparrow moved to Trinidad with his family when he was still a little boy. The talented musician composed songs at an early age. His first public performance was in 1954, when he was nineteen years old. Two years later, he won the Trinidad Carnival calypso competition with his song "Jean and Dinah." He has since composed innumerable songs and produced more than forty music albums.

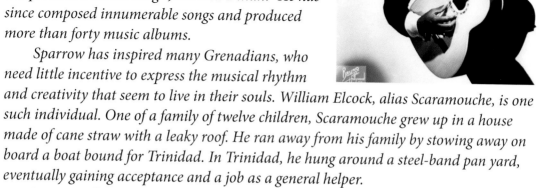

Sparrow has inspired many Grenadians, who need little incentive to express the musical rhythm and creativity that seem to live in their souls. William Elcock, alias Scaramouche, is one such individual. One of a family of twelve children, Scaramouche grew up in a house made of cane straw with a leaky roof. He ran away from his family by stowing away on board a boat bound for Trinidad. In Trinidad, he hung around a steel-band pan yard, eventually gaining acceptance and a job as a general helper.

Young William soon learned to play the steel drum—also known as playing pan—and became a professional, performing with a steel band. He also began to compose songs, eventually winning a calypso crown for one of his compositions. He joined the Mighty Sparrow and chose Scaramouche as his stage name because the film of that same title, starring Stewart Granger, was showing at the time. After a short sojourn in the United States, Scaramouche returned to Grenada in 1970 and won the country's calypso crown that year.

Another influential calypso and soca singer in Grenada was Alphonsus Cassell (1949–2010), a native of Montserrat better known as Arrow. He first learned to play the ukulele, then the guitar, and after that the steel drum. Arrow's trademark was his ability to improvise songs for the people he met. He believed this ability was a gift and said the lyrics just "came to him." Arrow performed at many hotel restaurants in Grenada's tourist belt, often accompanying himself on the guitar. During his career, he put out thirty albums.

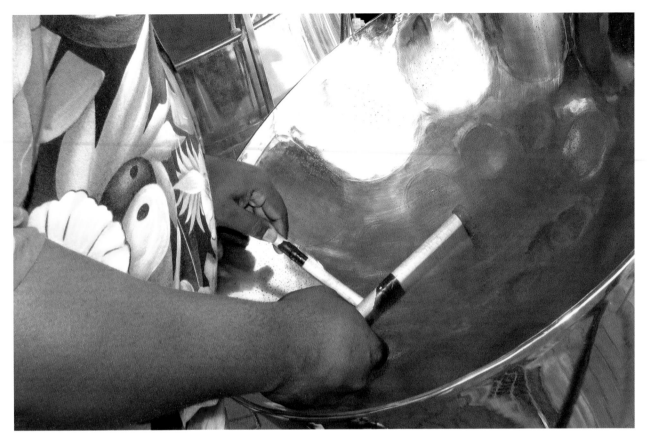

The music of a steel drum is one of the most distinctive sounds of the Caribbean.

of calypso, particularly suited for dancing—especially during Carnival. Soca produced in Grenada has a distinct style called "jab jab" soca.

MUSICAL INSTRUMENTS

The most distinctive musical instrument in Grenada is the pan, or steel drum. Like calypso, the pan originated in Trinidad, and it is an instrument born out of ingenuity and creativity. People were determined to make music even when the colonial authorities banned their traditional instruments. They found that the tops of discarded oil drums, which they retrieved from the garbage, could be coaxed into making music by "tuning" them, or beating them into shape.

The pan is the basic instrument of the steel band and is made from an oil drum with the bottom removed. The depth of the pan determines the instrument's range. After the bottom of the drum has been removed, the top is beaten into a concave shape divided into a number of sections separated by grooves that are chiseled into the surface. Each section is then beaten from the inside of the drum so that its surface is raised.

There are several types of pan: the ping-pong, or soprano, pan; the second, or alto, pan; the third, or tenor, pan; and the bass pan. Each pan is able to play the notes of the musical scale, and a good steel band can play a wide range of popular and classical music.

FOLK DANCES

Many of the Grenadian folk dances originated with African slavery, such as the *bongo* (BON-goh) and the *kalinda* (KA-lihn-dah). Both dances were traditionally performed at wakes in the belief that they helped the dead person transition from this world to the next. While the bongo has graceful movements, the kalinda resembles a choreographed stick fight.

The French and the English also contributed to the dance heritage of Grenada. The quadrille, a French dance popular in eighteenth-century England, was introduced to Grenada by the English. The quadrille was traditionally accompanied by tambourine, bass drum, violin, and triangle. At the end of the dance, it was the tradition to throw a bouquet, with the next quadrille gathering held in the home of the person who caught it. Although the quadrille is long gone in Europe, it survives in Carriacou.

Another French dance that arrived in Grenada via England was the lancers. It was performed by men dressed in tailcoats and frilled neckpieces and women in long flowing gowns.

The Africans developed the belair, a dance inspired by the quadrille and lancers. They performed this barefoot, and the women often wore bright headscarves with long-sleeve dresses and lacy petticoats, while the men had on headbands, colorful shirts, and white trousers.

WARM CLIMATE, VIBRANT COLORS

A typical house in Grenada is built up off the ground and painted a pretty color.

The Grenadian hillside is covered with small, square houses that have been built on pier foundations. As there is no need to insulate against the cold, the outdoors is brought into the living environment in the form of verandas, porches, balconies, and large windows with louvered shutters. At first, houses retained the natural hues of their building materials, but when paint became readily available, islanders used it to express their creativity on the exterior of their homes.

There are no basements in the houses. A series of steps usually leads the visitor up to the main door. The houses have one or two stories, and there are no high-rise buildings. Grenada prides itself on the fact that no building is allowed to be taller than a coconut palm.

There are many interesting historical buildings with distinctly European, especially French and English, architecture. The wrought-iron work along the Esplanade and Market Square in Saint George's is an example of French influence. The British influence is seen in the Georgian-style buildings.

FOLK ARTISTS

The history of art is relatively young in Grenada. In the twentieth century, many Grenadians took up painting, drawing, and sculpting. Most artists were self-taught painters who used watercolors and oils. Instead of canvas, which is not easily available on the island, hardboard and other types of fiberboard were used as surfaces. Paintings include scenes of island life—blue skies, clear waters, fishermen and their nets, market bustle, and children at play.

One well-known painter was Canute Caliste (1914—2005), who came from Carriacou. Known locally as CC or Old Head, he was eccentric and claimed to have been inspired as a child by a mermaid in Tyrrel Bay. After meeting her, he

UNDERWATER SCULPTURE PARK

Eerie figures haunt the ocean floor in the Molinière-Beauséjour Marine Protected Area off the coast of Saint George's. Sixty-five sculptures by British artist Jason deCaires Taylor reside there over a space of 8,611 square feet (800 sq m) of shallow seabed, about 16 to 26 feet (5 to 8 m) deep. Installed in 2006, it is the first of Taylor's undersea museums, as he calls them. As of 2019, he has built ten such submerged exhibits worldwide.

Vicissitudes (shown below), the signature piece in the Molinière park, depicts a circle of children holding hands. Cast from children of diverse ethnicities, the work is meant to be a symbol of unity and resilience.

All of the underwater sculptures, which are made from pH neutral cement and stainless steel, slowly become one with the natural environment. As coral polyps begin to grow on them, other sea life builds around them. In Grenada, the works are functioning as the bases for new coral reefs to help replace natural reefs that were damaged or destroyed during Hurricane Ivan. As the sea life grows on the artificial reefs, fish and other marine plants and animals are attracted to the region. Meanwhile, the artworks change over time, creating breathtaking, otherworldly scenes for the scuba diving tourists who visit them.

The painter Canute Caliste sits in front of his outdoor studio in Carriacou with his wife and grandchild in this photograph.

ran home to his mother, never went to school again, and didn't read or write, instead expressing himself through art and music. His paintings, described as "childlike" or "primitive," often featured mermaids in some way. He was also a self-taught fiddler who once played for Queen Elizabeth at Buckingham Palace.

FINE ARTS

Grenadian artworks are not all folksy, however. Contemporary artists like Stacey Byer, an abstract expressionist painter, want to change the perception that Grenadian art is all about beaches and sunsets. She uses vivid colors and heavy brushstrokes to invoke the culture of the Caribbean. She is one of Grenada's leading painters and illustrators, and she works to encourage female artists.

Grenadian artists are supported by the Grenada Arts Council, which organizes annual art shows. These shows provide many young artists an opportunity to exhibit their work outside of catering to the tourists' need for souvenirs. One young artist is Freddy Paul, who has become known in Grenada for his colorful and vibrant paintings. Paul is a watercolorist whose dream of having an art gallery has come true. He is self-taught and has won a number of awards.

GRENADIAN HANDICRAFTS

Grenadian handicrafts have a long history, beginning with the early settlers who arrived from South America. Excavations at Point Salines in the south of Grenada and at Duquesne Bay and Sauteurs in the north have unearthed finely crafted terra-cotta cooking pots and ceremonial vessels, intricate sculptures, arrowheads, and stone carvings.

The Grand Anse Craft and Spice Market is located on the famous Grand Anse Beach.

Today, many craftspeople make batik material; weave straw, bamboo, and wicker into hats, bags, and purses; carve furniture, kitchen utensils, and other useful and decorative household items out of mahogany, red cedar, and other woods; and make pieces out of coral and turtle shell.

The villagers of Marquis, on the eastern side of the main island, are known as expert weavers able to fashion all kinds of useful objects out of wild palm leaves.

THEATER AND LITERATURE

Grenadian theater began mainly as Shakespearean theater, a result of the English colonial period. Shakespearean plays were performed annually and on special occasions for the entertainment of the people. Many Grenadian actors got their start during this period. At the same time, there was theater based on folklore.

In the 1960s and 1970s, Grenadian playwrights became more inward looking and began to produce West Indian plays. Writers searched for a cultural identity, and oral poets performed in front of large crowds. Wilfred Redhead is an author from this period whose plays have been published and performed all over the Caribbean. His book *A City on a Hill* is a memoir of life in Saint George's.

Grenadian writer Omowale David Franklyn's book *Bridging the Two Grenadas* looks at the formation and transformation of Grenadian society and in particular the influence of two former prime ministers, Eric Gairy and Maurice Bishop.

Born in 1950, writer and scholar Merle Collins is considered Grenada's most distinguished writer today. She has published several novels and books of shorts stories and poetry. Her first collection of poetry, *Because the Dawn Breaks*, was published when she was a member of African Dawn, a group that performed poetry and mime to African music. Her other books of poetry as of 2019 are *Rotten Pomerack* and *Lady in a Boat*. A notable collection of stories, *The Ladies Are Upstairs*, was published in 2011.

In 2018, she was selected as the Distinguished Scholar Teacher of the Year at the University of Maryland, where she is a faculty member. In announcing the award, the university said, "Professor Merle Collins is an esteemed scholar, internationally acclaimed poet, ground-breaking oral archivist, highly regarded documentary film maker, and a brilliant teacher, who over the course of her career has become one of the most influential figures in the field of Anglophone Caribbean literature and culture."

INTERNET LINKS

https://www.bigdrumnation.com
Big Drum Nation is an online journal of Grenadian poetry, prose, visual art, criticism, bulletins, and interviews.

http://culture.gd
The Grenada Cultural Foundation has information about the arts

https://grenadaartscouncil.com
The Grenada Arts Council site profiles local artists.

https://grenadanationalarchives.wordpress.com/tag/grenadian-artists
The National Archives includes information about artists and musicians.

https://www.underwatersculpture.com
Jason deCaires Taylor's official site offers images and information about his underwater sculpture parks.

LEISURE

Young men play cricket on Gouyave Beach.

11

I N A BEAUTIFUL PLACE LIKE GRENADA, leisure seems almost mandatory as a lifestyle. With its tropical climate, beaches, mountains, and rain forests, it's a nature-lover's dream. This is what tourists travel to Grenada for, but the local people enjoy it as well. Grenadians love to have picnics by the sea or waterfalls and to hike through the beautiful mountain ranges in the center of the island.

Sports are a passion as well, for both the players and the fans. The British not only left Grenadians a legacy in their government, court, and education systems, but they also shared their love of soccer and cricket. Other leisure activities revolve around water, which is not surprising, since Grenada is surrounded by water and has a tropical climate.

Simple pleasures such as circle games continue to be passed down from generation to generation. Modern pastimes such as watching television have also pervaded the Grenadian lifestyle. With the growth of tourism, nightclubs have become a part of island life, and many residents now prefer to dance the night away.

CRICKET

Cricket was introduced to the English-speaking Caribbean region by the British, and Grenada has many excellent players. Cricket is played on an

Grenada's unofficial pastime is called liming. It's the art of doing nothing in the company of friends. It may involve some light conversation with food and drink, but it's mostly a matter of being peaceful, relaxing, and soaking in the outdoor beauty.

open green with two teams of eleven players each. The teams, whose players traditionally wear predominantly white uniforms, take turns trying to bat the ball and hit the wicket of the opposing team. The highest form of the game, with the longest match duration, is called Test cricket. This is the game played at many international championships, and matches can last for several days. However, One Day International (ODI) is a limited-duration form of cricket also played at the top level, and this format is used at the Cricket World Cup.

With their small populations, individual island nations like Grenada have difficulty producing enough excellent players to form national teams that can compete internationally. Grenadian cricketers vie with players from among other English-speaking Caribbean countries in competitions to select the best players to represent the West Indies in international championship games. Excitement runs particularly high when the West Indies plays against England.

Junior Murray (b. 1968) was lauded as Grenada's best cricket player during his career. He made sporting history when he became the first Grenadian to represent the West Indies in an international championship game. He has since retired from active play, but he serves as a coach. More recent Grenadian cricketers of note are Devon Smith, Andre Fletcher, and Rawl Lewis.

SOCCER

English football, or soccer, is another popular sport in Grenada. The Grenada Football Association has thirty-five member clubs that compete each year in the premier league. English football is played by two teams of eleven players each. A game lasts for ninety minutes, and the objective is for the teams to score as many goals as possible.

Grenada's national men's football team, flashy in their green, yellow, and red uniforms, is affectionately known as the Spice Boyz. The women footballers are the Spice Girlz. The most successful football club is generally thought to be the Hurricanes. They have won the Grenada National Championship more often than any other club, winning every year from 1969 to 1976. Jason Roberts, born in England to a Grenadian father and a Guyanese mother, has been called Grenada's most famous footballer. Although his home club is in Blackburn, England, he has played for Grenada in world football events. Shalrie Joseph,

The greatest sports hero in Grenada these days is track and field sprinter Kirani James (b. 1992). At the 2012 Summer Olympics in London, he became Grenada's first—and as of 2019, only—medal winner. That year, he won the gold medal in the 400-meter race, which is his specialty, and he nearly repeated that feat again at the 2016 Rio de Janeiro Games, when he won the silver. He's won a multitude of gold medals in other international championships. In 2012, James and Jamaica's star sprinter Usain Bolt were named co-sportsmen of the year by Caribbean Journal.

Grenada honored its hero with a commemorative stamp and named a new stadium for him. His birthday, September 1, is celebrated as Kirani Day. In 2017, James developed Graves disease, a thyroid disorder, and had to cut back on his athletic career.

Kirani James carrries the Grenada flag after placing third in the men's 400-meter final during the World Championships in Beijing, China, in 2015.

who played professional soccer in the United States on and off from 2003 to 2014, was named Grenada's Footballer of the Year in 2003. He served as the coach of Grenada's national team in the 2018—2019 season.

Every boys' school has cricket and football teams, and it is common to see young boys kicking a ball around on any available open ground. The fifteen-thousand-seat National Stadium, built in 2000 at a cost of $23 million, provides a prestigious venue for all major football and cricket games and track events on the island. It hosted some of the International Cricket Council (ICC) World Cup matches of 2007.

WATER SPORTS

There are numerous sailing events throughout the year, many hosted by the Grenada Yacht Club. They attract participants from all over the world. Every Easter, the Grenada Yacht Club

Kids play football (soccer) on a grassy lot in Saint George's.

holds a regatta where the main attraction is a race from Trinidad to Grenada. The Carriacou Regatta, which is held during a weekend in late July or early August, is a much bigger and older affair. It began in 1965 as a local boat race using traditional fishing boats and has evolved into a major Caribbean event, with keen competition among local sailors and those from neighboring islands.

Fishing, scuba diving, and snorkeling are other popular sports. There is good game fishing for marlin, sailfish, and yellowfin tuna. Anglers from all over the world, but especially from the United States and other Caribbean islands, compete in the Spice Island Billfish Tournament, which is held every January.

Grenada has some of the most beautiful beaches in the world, most famously Grand Anse. It is possible to wade into the sea and watch schools of fish in the clear blue waters. Even in the Carenage, an area where ships arrive every day to unload cargo, one can spot colorful reef fish. Coral reefs abound off the north, east, and south coasts of Grenada, off the east coasts of Carriacou and Petite Martinique, and around the smaller islands of the Grenadines. It is no wonder that these islands attract many snorkelers and divers.

OTHER LEISURE ACTIVITIES

On weekends, families often enjoy a picnic by the sea, a river, or a waterfall. Grenada has several lovely waterfalls: Concord and Annandale Falls in the parish of Saint John, Tufton Hall Waterfall in Saint Mark, and Saint Margaret Falls in the heart of Grand Etang National Park.

A traditional Grenadian picnic is a simple affair. Almost everything that is required for a meal is available on the spot. Three stones form a triangle on which a pot is put, dry twigs and branches are placed underneath, and a fire is lit. Bowls, hollowed out of calabash shells, are the only containers needed, and a spoon can be quickly fashioned out of a twig.

Hiking is another activity accessible to all. The central mountains, especially those in Grand Etang National Park, have many well-developed nature trails. Mount Qua Qua provides the hiker with a wonderful view of the surrounding countryside. Some people love to hunt. They shoot monkeys and armadillos. Some consider the meat of these animals a delicacy.

A daring young man jumps from the top of Concord Falls, a popular tourist attraction.

CHILDREN'S GAMES

Circle games were popular in the past. Two well-known examples of circle games that have come to us from the Caribbean are Brown Girl in the Ring and Here We Go Loop-de-Lou. These song games were played in schoolyards, at home with friends, or with parents and elders who taught the art of singing to the young.

In Carriacou, similar songs called pass plays were sung by a circle of adults, most notably at wakes. Another is a kalinda, or stick-fighting, song. The stickman and his supporters sing a challenge to all to "meet me on the road."

Today, children spend their time cycling with friends, playing soccer and basketball, or pitching marbles. Girls enjoy jumping rope and playing jacks, baseball, and hopscotch. A popular game called *morual* (MOR-u-al) involves drawing a rectangle in the dirt and dividing it into eight or ten sections. A ball is thrown, and the players move through the sections, trying to gain control of as many as possible.

Some families gather in the living room to relax and watch television. If a home is without a television set, time is spent reading a book or talking and relaxing with friends under the shade of a large tree.

RELAXING WITH RUM

Men like to get together with their friends at the local rum shop for a "happy hour" of "eights" and a game of dominoes or cards. An "eight" is a measure of rum that is often drunk in one gulp or consumed a little more slowly and shared among friends. If one desires, the rum can be washed down with a glass of iced water. Dominoes is a game that is taken seriously in Grenada. Men form clubs that compete in a championship.

NIGHTLIFE

Nightlife in Grenada is picking up due to the increasing emphasis on tourism. Most hotels and resorts have their own clubs catering to tourists and locals alike. These places offer live entertainment with dancing, drumming, and steel bands. The steel bands play soca, reggae, and other Caribbean music. Besides catering to the needs of the local population, these places offer tourists a cultural cabaret, a chance to sample a little of the local culture and folklore.

FOLKTALES

Storytelling is a very important tradition in Grenada that springs from African roots. Folktales are a means of teaching people about their past, their culture, and the values of their society.

Story time often begins with someone calling out "Tim tim" or "Crick crack," to which the children respond with "Papa welcome" or whatever the local custom happens to be. Then, everyone gathers around to listen to famous stories about Anansi. Half-man, half-spider, Anansi is cunning, greedy, and shrewd.

In the Anansi stories, small and seemingly weak animals are able to overcome strong and threatening ones such as tigers and pythons by their wit and trickery. It is customary for the storyteller to finish by announcing, "The story end and wire bend." The children are then treated to some food or drink. The Anansi stories, an African tradition, come from the days of slavery, when the art of storytelling brought great comfort to an oppressed people.

INTERNET LINKS

https://www.goatsontheroad.com/61-things-do-grenada
This travel site lists numerous leisure activities and destinations, with links and videos.

https://www.nowgrenada.com/category/sports
Up-to-date sports news for Grenada can be found on this site.

FESTIVALS

A lavishly-costumed dancer takes part in the
Carnival festivities in Saint George's.

12

GRENADIAN FESTIVITIES ARE MARKED by great feasting, laughter, music, and dancing that last throughout the day. Being an island nation, many of the celebrations relate to fishing and sailing. Regattas of all sorts take place annually, and the town of Gouyave, for example, marks every Friday as Fish Friday. Vendors sell all manner of fresh seafood, and outdoor feasting is accompanied by music and fun.

With its Christian heritage, Grenada observes all the major church holidays, such as Easter and Christmas. Its national festival, Carnival, grows out of that heritage but now incorporates African and Caribbean heritage as well.

CARNIVAL

Historically, Carnival allowed people to have a big celebration before Lent, the season leading up to Easter when they were required to fast. Carnival was their last chance to dance, sing, and make merry before the forty days of the somber Lenten season.

When Grenada was a French colony, the planters celebrated this time with much socializing. They had dinners and concerts and paraded in beautiful costumes. After emancipation in 1834, former slaves used

Although Carnival is celebrated throughout the Caribbean, Grenada's Carnival, Spicemas, is different. It takes place in August rather than during the usual February. It also incorporates its own spooky element of Jab Jab J'ouvert. In the predawn hours leading to the first day of Carnival, thousands of masqueraded *jab jabs* (horned devils coated in glistening oil) take to the streets to start the festivities.

Members of the Saint George's Girl Guides sing carols at Christmastime in the city.

Christmas is a joyous time. Houses are thoroughly cleaned, new things replace the old, and everybody dresses in his or her best clothes to go visiting. Musicians go around caroling or serenading. Kitchens bustle with the enormous amount of cooking that needs to be done to ensure that all who pass by or step in the door are fed to their heart's content. Also, it wouldn't be Christmas in Grenada without black Christmas cake, a traditional dark, spicy fruitcake of rum-soaked fruits.

PARANG

Parang, a festival that occurs the weekend before Christmas, is unique to Carriacou. Parang came to Grenada from South America via Trinidad. It grew

A YEAR OF CELEBRATION

The following days are public holidays in Grenada. Schools and many businesses are closed. Dates that are not specified are moveable feasts, including Christian observances related to Easter and its aftermath, and Carnival, which takes place on the second Monday and Tuesday of August.

January 1 . . . . *New Year's Day*
February 7 . . . . . . *Independence Day*
March or April . . . . *Good Friday*
                        Easter Sunday
                        Easter Monday
May 1 . . . . *Labor Day*
May or June . . . . . *Pentecost, or Whit Sunday*
May or June . . . . . *Corpus Christi*
August 5 . . . . *Emancipation Day*
August . . . . *Carnival (Monday and Tuesday)*
October 25 . . . . . . *Thanksgiving*
December 25 . . . . . *Christmas Day*
December 26 . . . . . *Boxing Day*

out of the tradition of going from house to house caroling. Today, it is less a celebration of Christmas and has an identity of its own.

Parang songs are sung in English. Full of humor, the songs are often impromptu and tell of someone's misdeeds. The festival was started in 1977 by the Mount Royal Progressive Youth Movement, a nonprofit organization that wanted to celebrate this aspect of the island's culture. Bands playing only percussion instruments sing about political and other talked-about events of the year. If one does something scandalous, especially close to the month of December, one might be warned to "be careful, we go put you on the banjo!" Most songs are sung with a biting humor. Names are sometimes linked with the rumors sung in the Parang songs.

The three-day festival begins with a Hosanna Bands contest—a carol-singing contest among village groups. This is followed by a calypso and soca jam session. Performers from Carriacou and other parts of Grenada entertain a large crowd, and foreign artists are usually invited. Festivities reach a climax on the third night, when Parang groups compete for the challenge trophy and other prizes. Traditional Carriacou dances such as the quadrille add to the festivities.

BIG DRUM

Carriacou is particularly known for Big Drum. The festival is experiencing a revival, especially as young Carriacouans are renewing their interest in their heritage of African drumming and dances.

Big Drum music uses three drums. The center drum is called the cot drum; the two side drums are bula drums. Dancers and singers accompany the drums. The lead singer sings parables of repression, warfare, and other troubles, or tales of gossip. Some songs tell of a longing for West Africa, while others lament the lives of the people or ridicule the oppressors. Dancers are called forth by the beat of the drum, and they dance in a circle. The dances reflect the African heritage of the various peoples who came to the island—the Kromanti, the Ibo, the Mandingo, the Chamba, the Banda, the Moko, and others. The Kromanti dance is the most significant because the Kromanti, originally from Ghana, were one of the first groups to come to Carriacou. Every ceremony opens and closes with the Kromanti dance.

MAROON

Associated with the Big Drum Festival is Maroon, an especially big sacrificial feast. Each year, for the Dumfries Maroon in Carriacou, several families, often related, will prepare food that is put on trays and then placed on both sides of the road leading to Dumfries. Some food is taken from each tray by specially appointed people and presented to the Big Drum participants who will perform in the evening. The rest of the food is offered to passersby.

BOAT-LAUNCHING FESTIVAL

Boatbuilding has a long and important history on Carriacou, so there is a celebration when a new boat is to be launched. The ceremony begins with a Big Drum performance and a saraca feast, followed by the pouring of spirits and the sprinkling of rice around the boat. Animals are ritually slaughtered. Chickens are killed in the galley to symbolize an abundance of food, a ram is killed on the stern to bless the ship with fair winds, and a sheep is slaughtered over the bow to make steering easy. A second round of spirits is then poured around the boat.

A priest is usually invited to bless the boat. He says his prayers and sprinkles holy water over the boat while accompanied by two people who represent the godparents of the boat. The culmination of the ceremony is the unfurling of a flag with the boat's name. Then, as the drums roll, there is the important "cutting down" of the boat. Men all along the side of the boat use axes to cut the posts on which it rests, and the boat is gradually lowered into the sea.

INTERNET LINKS

https://www.huffpost.com/entry/inside-grenadas-spicemas-a -caribbean-carnival-of_b_59a62028e4b05fa16286be33
The color and fun of Spicemas is described in this travel article.

https://www.timeanddate.com/holidays/grenada
This calendar site provides yearly listings of Grenada's holidays and observances.

FOOD

Cocoa pods and beans are artfully displayed. Cocoa trees were introduced to Grenada in 1714, and the beans have since been an important export. The island didn't start making its own chocolate, however, until 1999.

LIKE ALL CARIBBEAN CUISINE, Grenadian cooking is influenced by many cultures. African, Spanish, British, Dutch, French, Portuguese, Chinese, and East Indian fare are all reflected in the cuisine. Grenadians have been able to match this rich heritage with a plentiful variety of fresh foods for the cooking pot. Add spices—for Grenada is known as the Isle of Spice—and the result is a cuisine that is varied, interesting, and unique to the country.

GROUND PROVISIONS

While the potato is a staple food in Grenadian cooking, "ground provisions" are a popular substitute. Dasheens, tannias, eddoes, yams, cassavas, and sweet potatoes may be steamed, boiled, or added to stews. There are also two members of the banana family that are equally versatile—the plantain, which looks like a large green banana, and the bluggoe, which is shorter and thicker in size. These rather starchy, solid, and bland fruits are often fried and eaten as a snack.

Another starchy item that often makes its appearance on the dinner table is breadfruit. This round, green fruit is cooked and eaten like a

Slavery left an important imprint on the country's cooking. The enslaved African people could not afford meat or fish. Instead, they resorted to cooking with "ground provisions"—starchy root vegetables, such as cassavas, yams, dasheens, and sweet potatoes. Beans, salt fish, and salt pork added some variety to their diet. Ground provisions remain an important part of the Grenadian diet today.

vegetable. Breadfruit is native to the Pacific Islands, and the story is that it was introduced in the late eighteenth century to provide food for the slaves. It is bland and chewy, but it absorbs the flavors of the spices with which it is cooked. Breadfruit balls are made by mashing the breadfruit, forming it into balls, and deep-frying them. Breadfruit soup is made with salted meat and onions. Grenada's national dish, oil down, is made with breadfruit and meat, usually chicken or pork, cooked in coconut milk. A kind of heavy dumpling is added to the stew. Turmeric produces the characteristic yellow color of the dish.

OIL DOWN

Grenadians cook lots of soups and stews. The national dish of Grenada, oil down, is a stew of meat, vegetables, and dumplings cooked in coconut milk. Although recipes differ, the spicy stew typically includes salted fish or meat, breadfruit, hot peppers, callaloo leaves, onions, and carrots. The dish is called an "oil down" because after cooking, the coconut milk boils down, leaving an oil that soaks into the breadfruit. "Oil down" is also the name of an outdoor party featuring the stew and other dishes.

ROTI AND RICE

When the Europeans arrived, they introduced new foods and drinks—wine, olive oil, cheese, salami, and European spices. They also brought bread. Slaves were taught by their planter families to make bread, but being used to ground provisions, they made a heavier kind of bread. Today, bread is found in many forms but most commonly as a kind of long roll or "French" bread, with a crusty surface. Bakeries also make buns and butter bread—French rolls made of a heavy, unleavened dough—as well as a lighter version leavened with yeast. People drop by the bakeries during the day to buy not only bread but also drinks and "pies," which are squares or triangles of pastry filled with meat, fish, salami, cheese, or jam.

After slavery was abolished, new groups of indentured laborers arrived in the region and brought with them more new foods. The East Indians introduced curry powder and a thin pancake made of flour and water, called a roti. The Chinese brought Asian spices and vegetables.

Grenadians have transformed the Indian roti and curry into something of their own. The pancake is made into a wrap and filled with a curry-flavored potato-and-meat mixture that is a meal in itself.

Rice, which was probably introduced by the East Indian and Chinese communities, is also popular. It is often cooked with pigeon peas, also called yellow peas. Alternatively, rice is cooked with spices and is then known as seasoning rice. Pigeon peas may also be served on their own as a side dish or cooked with salt beef and other meats and seasonings.

OTHER FAVORITE DISHES

A soup commonly found in restaurants is the thick, dark-green callaloo soup. The callaloo is the tender leaf of the dasheen plant, and it looks and tastes like spinach. It is simmered in coconut milk and spices until soft.

Souse is a festive dish made with pig's feet. The feet are cleaned and boiled until tender. The meat is then sliced and combined with a sauce made from garlic, onions, lime juice, salt, and pepper. Curry goat is a popular stew, served with rice and mango chutney. Seafood is often served for dinner. Conch, or *lambi* (LAM-bi), is the most popular seafood delicacy.

Grenadian food, though well spiced and seasoned, is seldom chili-hot, although the Caribbean is home to one of the world's hottest peppers, the Scotch bonnet. Though dishes are not made to be spicy, nearly every restaurant table will have a bottle of hot sauce on it.

Favorite desserts include nutmeg ice cream and sweet potato pone, a baked pudding.

A bowl of callaloo soup is garnished with grilled bacon.

ISLE OF SPICE

No discussion of Grenadian food can be complete without mentioning spices. The island is known as the Isle of Spice for good reason. All kinds are grown here: cloves, cinnamon, ginger, vanilla, bay, turmeric (which Grenadians call saffron), pimento, pepper, nutmeg, and mace. These are used in many combinations to flavor all sorts of meat dishes, cakes, and sweets.

Chicken, pork, beef, and mutton are all part of the Grenadian diet. These are marinated with spices and cooked slowly. Marinating and seasoning are important elements in Grenadian cooking. Except for tender cuts of meat and quick-cooking foods such as fish, hardly anything is cooked without being properly seasoned and marinated for a few hours. The secret of spicing the food is to ensure that the taste of the individual spices do not stand out; rather, the spices should combine to produce a subtle blend of flavors.

The spices of "The Spice Isle" are for sale at a market in Grenada.

The West Indies believes that it produces the world's hottest pepper, the Scotch bonnet. However, it is facing competition from the bhutjolokia, which comes from India. Even if it has been toppled from the topmost rung of the fire ladder, the Scotch bonnet is a pepper to be treated with great respect. It is many times hotter than the jalapeño and the serrano,

two peppers commonly found in North American stores. Its name comes from the crinkled crown of the pepper, which some believe looks like a traditional Scottish bonnet. There are red, yellow, orange, and green ones. The hottest part of the pepper is not the seeds, as some people believe, but the white veins, which contain the capsaicin, the substance responsible for the fiery power of the vegetable.

It is difficult to understand what it is that makes the heat of the pepper such an attraction for people who live in hot countries. One theory is that it fosters perspiration, which is the body's natural cooling mechanism. Another is that there is a "high" that comes from eating hot peppers that makes those who love it want more. The body reacts to the pain caused by eating the peppers by producing endorphins, the same natural compounds that produce the so-called runner's high.

Early European explorers found that if sailors ate peppers during long sea voyages, they did not suffer from scurvy. Peppers are rich in vitamins A and C.

REFRESHING DRINKS

Fruit juices abound in Grenada: mango, papaya, golden apple (called June plum in other parts of the Caribbean), orange, avocado, guava, passion fruit, lime, banana, five-finger fruit (also known as carambola or starfruit), soursop, and sweetsop (or custard apple), to name a few.

Grenadians make juice with the most unlikely of ingredients. Even the sour tamarind is made into a deliciously tart drink. Ginger beer, which is nonalcoholic, is also extremely popular. Mawby is made by boiling pieces of a tree native to the Caribbean together with some orange peel and spices. This produces a dark bitter liquid that is diluted, sweetened, and left to ferment for a few days. The resulting drink is reminiscent of licorice, leaving a lingering and slightly bitter, herbal aftertaste. Sea moss is a milky sweet drink made from seaweed.

Sorrel is drunk during the Christmas season. It is made from the fleshy dark-red sepals of a small plant from the hibiscus family that is also native to the Caribbean. The sepals are picked and soaked in water with bay leaves, cloves, and cinnamon, and then they are strained to make a dark-colored drink. The plant flowers only around December.

A common scene in the markets is that of vendors slashing off the tops of coconuts. Coconut juice is popular with shoppers who, after some hours of shopping under the blazing sun, like to enjoy this cooling drink in the shade.

A delicious warm drink is cocoa tea, made by steeping cocoa balls in hot water with sweetened milk. Cocoa balls are made from grated cocoa with herbs and spices such as cinnamon, thyme, and bay leaf.

A refreshing glass of golden ginger beer is garnished with lime and mint.

RUM

Rum is the alcoholic drink that is most associated with the Caribbean. Rum is produced from sugarcane, and there are as many kinds of rum as there are islands in the region. There are several rum distilleries on Grenada Island.

The color of rum ranges from almost colorless to a dark brown. A light-colored rum is aged in ordinary oak casks, while a darker rum is aged in charred-oak casks. Sugar caramel is sometimes added for color. Rum is also used in cooking, baking, and many cocktail concoctions. One concoction is rum punch, a drink that can be traced back to plantation days.

A worker operates a sugarcane press at the River Antoine Rum Distillery in Grenada. The distillery dates to 1785 and has the oldest working water wheel (shown here) in the Caribbean.

INTERNET LINKS

https://www.carnival.com/awaywego/travel/caribbean/top-13-things-to-eat-in-grenada
This travel company suggests Grenadian dishes to try.

http://culture.gd/index.php/oc/food
This Grenadian culture site includes recipes for traditional dishes.

OIL DOWN

The national dish of Grenada uses ingredients that are hard to find in most US grocery stores. This simplified recipe offers suggestions for substitutions. Caribbean-style dumplings called "spinners" are often added to an oil down.

1 pound salted meat (ham, unsliced bacon, or salt pork—authentic additions would include pig snouts and pig tails) *and/or* pre-soaked salt cod *and/or* 4 chicken pieces, such as thighs and drumsticks

1 large green breadfruit (about 2 pounds) (substitute peeled plantains and/or potatoes)

2 medium onions, sliced

2 stalks celery, chopped

2 carrots, peeled and chopped (optional)

3 chili peppers, chopped (optional)

2 large sprigs thyme

8–10 dasheen (callaloo) leaves (substitute ½ pound spinach or chard)

2 cups coconut milk

2 tsp turmeric

This stew is assembled in layers.

Cut meat into pieces. Place in a large, heavy stew pot. Add fish and/or chicken, if using.

Peel the skin of the breadfruit. Cut into 4 or 5 vertical wedges. Remove center core. Cut wedges crosswise into chunks. Arrange breadfruit pieces on the meat.

Top with onion, celery, and thyme—and carrots and chilis, if using.

Remove thick stems from dasheen (or spinach or chard) leaves. Spread leaves on top of the breadfruit.

Add the coconut milk and turmeric. Cover the pot tightly, bring to a simmer, then lower heat to medium. Cook until all the liquid is absorbed.

Serve with slices of avocado.

NUTMEG ICE CREAM

This recipe is best made using an ice cream maker.

Special equipment: candy thermometer, ice cream maker

1 ½ cups whole milk

1 ½ cups heavy cream

3 large eggs

¾ cup sugar

1 Tbsp grated fresh nutmeg (about
   1 whole nutmeg; do not substitute
   powdered nutmeg)

⅛ tsp salt

1 ½ tsp vanilla extract

In a saucepan, bring the milk and cream just to a boil. Immediately turn off the heat as soon as bubbles appear. Set aside.

In a medium-size bowl, whisk together the eggs, sugar, nutmeg, salt, and vanilla.

Whisk ½ cup of the milk mixture into the egg mixture, and then pour the egg mixture into the remaining milk mixture in the saucepan, whisking constantly.

Cook the custard over moderate heat, stirring constantly with a wooden spoon, until it registers 175 degrees Fahrenheit (79.5 degrees Celsius) on a candy thermometer.

Transfer the custard to a metal bowl set in a larger bowl of ice and cold water and stir until the custard is cold.

Freeze the custard in an ice-cream maker according to the manufacturer's instructions. Alternatively, pour the mixture into a freezer-safe dish and freeze, stirring vigorously by hand or with an electric mixer every 30 minutes until it is completely frozen (about 2 hours).

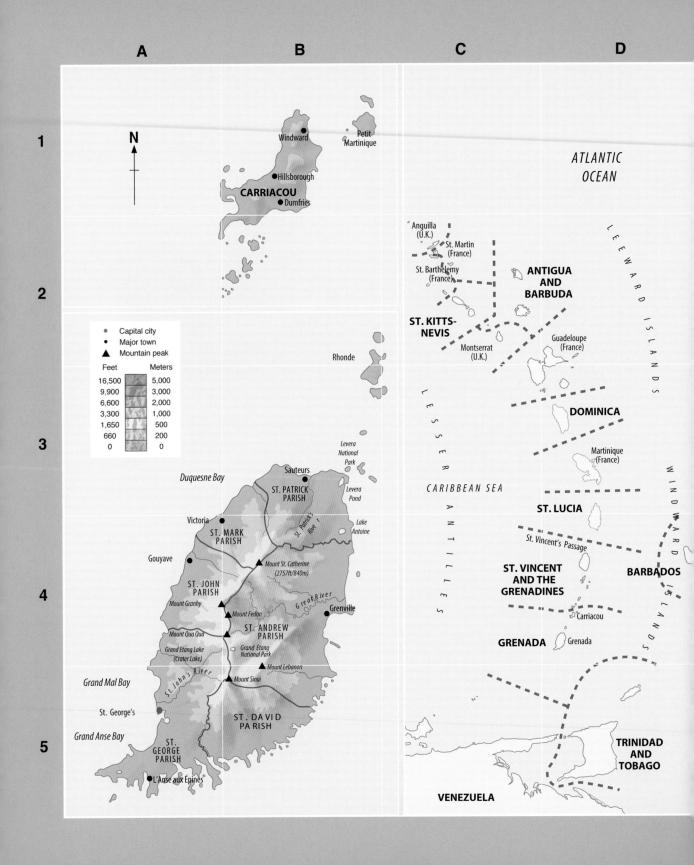

A **B** **C** **D**

1

N

Windward

Petit
Martinique

Hillsborough

CARRIACOU

Dumfries

ATLANTIC
OCEAN

2

Anguilla
(U.K.)

St. Martin
(France)

St. Barthélemy
(France)

**ANTIGUA
AND
BARBUDA**

**ST. KITTS-
NEVIS**

Montserrat
(U.K.)

Guadeloupe
(France)

Rhonde

● Capital city
● Major town
▲ Mountain peak

Feet		Meters
16,500		5,000
9,900		3,000
6,600		2,000
3,300		1,000
1,650		500
660		200
0		0

3

Levera
National
Park

Duquesne Bay

Sauteurs

**ST. PATRICK
PARISH**

Levera
Pond

Victoria

Lake
Antoine

**ST. MARK
PARISH**

DOMINICA

Martinique
(France)

CARIBBEAN SEA

ST. LUCIA

St. Vincent's Passage

4

Gouyave

▲ Mount St. Catherine
(2757ft/840m)

**ST. JOHN
PARISH**

Mount Granby

▲ Mount Fedon

**ST. ANDREW
PARISH**

Mount Qua Qua ▲

Grand Etang Lake
(Crater Lake)

Grand Etang
National Park

▲ Mount Lebanon

▲ Mount Sinai

Grenville

**ST. VINCENT
AND THE
GRENADINES**

BARBADOS

Carriacou

GRENADA ● Grenada

Grand Mal Bay

St. George's

Grand Anse Bay

**ST.
GEORGE
PARISH**

**ST. DAVID
PARISH**

5

L'Anse aux Épines

VENEZUELA

**TRINIDAD
AND
TOBAGO**

Great River

St. John's River

St. Patrick's River

MAP OF GRENADA

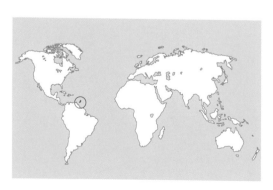

ECONOMIC GRENADA

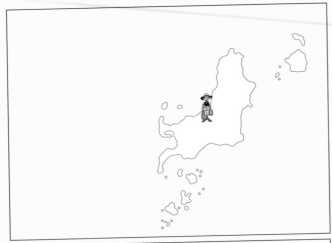

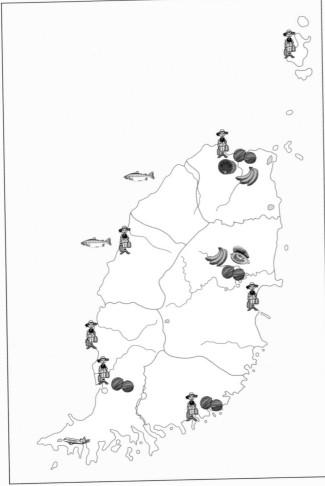

Services

 Airport

 Tourism

Agriculture

Bananas

Cocoa

Nutmeg

Manufacturing

 Rum distilling

Natural Resources

 Fishing

ABOUT THE ECONOMY

All figures are 2017 estimates unless otherwise noted.

GROSS DOMESTIC PRODUCT (GDP, OFFICIAL EXCHANGE RATE)
$1.119 billion

GDP BY SECTOR OF ORIGIN
Agriculture: 6.8 percent
Industry: 15.5 percent
Services: 77.7 percent

INFLATION RATE
0.9 percent

LABOR FORCE
55,270

UNEMPLOYMENT RATE
24 percent

POPULATION BELOW POVERTY LINE
38 percent

CURRENCY
1 East Caribbean dollar (XCD) = 100 cents
US$1 = 2.70 XCD (July 2019)

AGRICULTURAL PRODUCTS
bananas, cocoa, nutmeg, mace, soursop, citrus, avocados, root crops, corn, vegetables, fish

INDUSTRIES
food and beverages, textiles, light assembly operations, tourism, construction, education, call-center operations

MAJOR IMPORTS
food, manufactured goods, machinery, chemicals, fuel

MAJOR EXPORTS
nutmeg, bananas, cocoa, fruit and vegetables, clothing, mace, chocolate, fish

TRADE PARTNERS
United States, Trinidad and Tobago, Japan, Guyana, China, Dominica, Saint Lucia, Netherlands, Barbados, Saint Kitts and Nevis

CULTURAL GRENADA

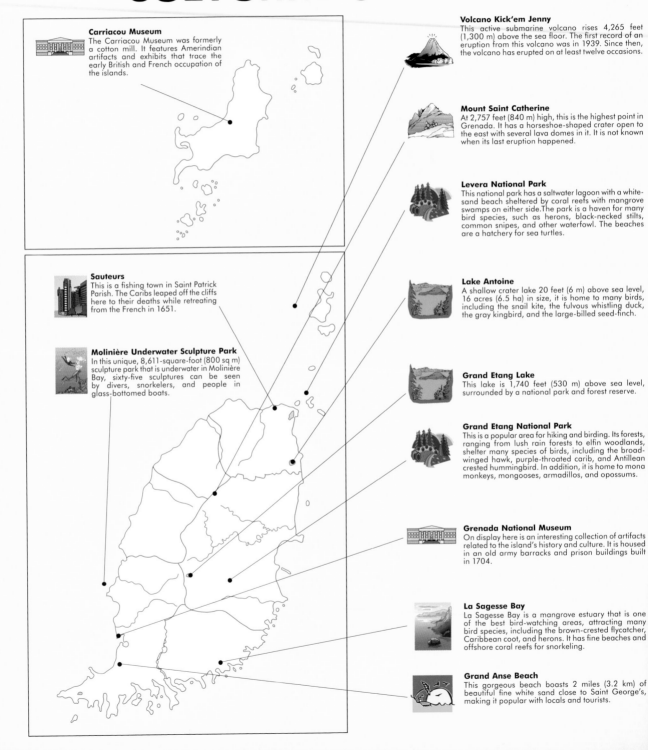

Carriacou Museum
The Carriacou Museum was formerly a cotton mill. It features Amerindian artifacts and exhibits that trace the early British and French occupation of the islands.

Sauteurs
This is a fishing town in Saint Patrick Parish. The Caribs leaped off the cliffs here to their deaths while retreating from the French in 1651.

Molinière Underwater Sculpture Park
In this unique, 8,611-square-foot (800 sq m) sculpture park that is underwater in Molinière Bay, sixty-five sculptures can be seen by divers, snorkelers, and people in glass-bottomed boats.

Volcano Kick'em Jenny
This active submarine volcano rises 4,265 feet (1,300 m) above the sea floor. The first record of an eruption from this volcano was in 1939. Since then, the volcano has erupted on at least twelve occasions.

Mount Saint Catherine
At 2,757 feet (840 m) high, this is the highest point in Grenada. It has a horseshoe-shaped crater open to the east with several lava domes in it. It is not known when its last eruption happened.

Levera National Park
This national park has a saltwater lagoon with a white-sand beach sheltered by coral reefs with mangrove swamps on either side. The park is a haven for many bird species, such as herons, black-necked stilts, common snipes, and other waterfowl. The beaches are a hatchery for sea turtles.

Lake Antoine
A shallow crater lake 20 feet (6 m) above sea level, 16 acres (6.5 ha) in size, it is home to many birds, including the snail kite, the fulvous whistling duck, the gray kingbird, and the large-billed seed-finch.

Grand Etang Lake
This lake is 1,740 feet (530 m) above sea level, surrounded by a national park and forest reserve.

Grand Etang National Park
This is a popular area for hiking and birding. Its forests, ranging from lush rain forests to elfin woodlands, shelter many species of birds, including the broad-winged hawk, purple-throated carib, and Antillean crested hummingbird. In addition, it is home to mona monkeys, mongooses, armadillos, and opossums.

Grenada National Museum
On display here is an interesting collection of artifacts related to the island's history and culture. It is housed in an old army barracks and prison buildings built in 1704.

La Sagesse Bay
La Sagesse Bay is a mangrove estuary that is one of the best bird-watching areas, attracting many bird species, including the brown-crested flycatcher, Caribbean coot, and herons. It has fine beaches and offshore coral reefs for snorkeling.

Grand Anse Beach
This gorgeous beach boasts 2 miles (3.2 km) of beautiful fine white sand close to Saint George's, making it popular with locals and tourists.

ABOUT THE CULTURE

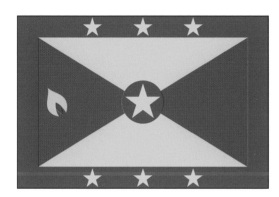

All figures are 2018 estimates unless otherwise noted.

OFFICIAL NAME
Grenada

CAPITAL
Saint George's

LAND AREA
140 square miles (363 sq km)

COASTLINE
75 miles (121 km)

ADMINISTRATIVE DIVISIONS
Six parishes—Saint Andrew, Saint David, Saint George, Saint John, Saint Mark, and Saint Patrick—and the dependencies of Carriacou and Petite Martinique

ANTHEM
"Hail Grenada"

LANGUAGE
English (official), French Patois

NATIONAL BIRD
The Grenada dove

NATIONAL FLOWER
Bougainvillea

POPULATION
112,207

POPULATION GROWTH RATE
0.42 percent

ETHNIC GROUPS
African descent 82.4 percent, mixed 13.3 percent, East Indian 2.2 percent, other 1.3 percent, unspecified 0.9 percent (2011)

MAJOR RELIGIONS
Protestant 49.2 percent (includes Pentecostal 17.2 percent, Seventh Day Adventist 13.2 percent, Anglican 8.5 percent, Baptist 3.2 percent, Church of God 2.4 percent, Evangelical 1.9 percent, Methodist 1.6 percent, other 1.2 percent), Roman Catholic 36 percent, Jehovah's Witness 1.2 percent, Rastafarian 1.2 percent, other 5.5 percent, none 5.7 percent, unspecified 1.3 percent (2011)

LIFE EXPECTANCY AT BIRTH
Total population: 74.8 years
Male: 72.1 years
Female: 77.6 years

LITERACY RATE
98.6 percent (2014)

TIMELINE

IN GRENADA	IN THE WORLD

1–1000 CE
Arawaks make Grenada their home.

1000
The Chinese perfect gunpowder and begin to use it in warfare.

1000–1650
Caribs live on Grenada.

1498
Columbus sees the island of Grenada.

1530
Beginning of transatlantic slave trade is organized by the Portuguese in Africa.

1609
First attempted settlement made by British merchants.

1638
French try to establish a settlement on Grenada.

1650
Jacques-Dyel du Parquet, French governor of Martinique, purchases Grenada Island.

1651–1652
French wage war against the Caribs.

1763
France cedes Grenada to the British as part of the Treaty of Paris.

1776
US Declaration of Independence is written.

1779
French recapture Grenada.

1783
Grenada is restored to British rule in accordance with the Treaty of Versailles.

1789–1799
The French Revolution takes place.

1795
Failed rebellion by African planter Julien Fedon takes place.

1834
Slavery is abolished.

1914
World War I begins.

1939
World War II begins.

1945
The United States drops atomic bombs on Japan. World War II ends.

1958
Grenada becomes part of the Federation of the West Indies.

IN GRENADA		IN THE WORLD
1967		
Grenada becomes autonomous, with foreign and defense affairs remaining under British control.		**1969** US astronaut Neil Armstrong becomes first human on the moon.
1974 Grenada gains independence.		
1979 Prime Minster Eric Gairy is ousted in a coup; People's Revolutionary Government under Maurice Bishop takes over.		
1983 Bishop is executed; coup sparks US invasion of Grenada.		**1991** Breakup of the Soviet Union occurs.
1995 Keith Mitchell serves first term as prime minister.		**2001** Terrorists stage 9/11 attacks in United States.
2004 Hurricane Ivan devastates 90 percent of Grenada.		**2003** War in Iraq begins.
2005 Hurricane Emily destroys much of Grenada.		
2008 Former prime minister Sir Eric Gairy is named as the country's first National Hero.		**2008** US elects first African American president, Barack Obama. **2009** Outbreak of H1N1 flu spreads around the world.
2012 Sprinter Kirani James wins Grenada's first Olympic medal.		
2013 The New National Party wins a landslide victory in parliamentary elections. Keith Mitchell returns as prime minister.		**2015–2016** ISIS launches terror attacks in Belgium and France. **2017** Donald Trump becomes US president. Hurricanes devastate Houston, Caribbean islands, and Puerto Rico.
2018 Mitchell's party again wins by a landslide; Mitchell continues as prime minister until 2023.		
2019 Grenada celebrates fortieth anniversary of Grenada Revolution with concert and exhibitions.		**2019** Terrorist attacks mosques in New Zealand. Notre Dame Cathedral in Paris is damaged by fire.

GLOSSARY

Amerindians
The original people who inhabited the Americas.

animism
The belief that spirits inhabit natural objects such as stones and trees.

calypso
A style of Afro-Caribbean music that originated in Trinidad, characterized by highly rhythmic and harmonic vocals.

creole
Also called patois, a language that is based on two or more languages.

jab jab (JAB-jab)
A creole word for "devil."

Lajabless
A devil woman.

lambi (LAM-bi)
The Grenadian word for "conch."

liming
The art of doing nothing, with someone else.

obeah
A type of African witchcraft.

oil down
The Grenadian national dish, a stew of meats and vegetables cooked with coconut milk.

pan
A percussion instrument made from an oil drum, essential to a steel band. Also called a steel drum.

petroglyphs
Prehistoric drawings or carvings on rock.

playing mas
Dressing up in costumes and masks during Carnival.

Rastafarianism
A religion that teaches that Haile Selassie, a former emperor of Ethiopia, was God and that black people must return to their home, Africa, one day.

saraca (SAH-ra-ca)
A sacrificial feast.

Shango
An African religion that features a belief in many spirits.

soca
A genre of music that grew out of calypso. The term "soca" comes from the phrase "soul of calypso."

Spicemas
Grenada's preeminent carnival, which takes place each August.

FOR FURTHER INFORMATION

BOOKS

Buffong, Jean. *Under the Silk Cotton Tree*. Northampton, MA: Interlink Publishing Group, 1993.

Crask, Paul. *Grenada, Carriacou, and Petite Martinique*. Chalfont St. Peter, UK: Bradt Travel Guides, 2018.

Marcus, Bruce, and Michael Taber. *Maurice Bishop Speaks: The Grenada Revolution and Its Overthrow 1979—83*. New York, NY: Pathfinder Press, 1983.

O'Shaughnessy, Hugh. *Grenada: An Eyewitness Account of the U.S. Invasion and the Caribbean History That Provoked It*. New York, NY: Dodd Mead, 1985.

Victor, Teddy. *Deception on Conception: What Happened in Grenada 1962—1990*. Huntington, WV: Publishers Place, Inc., 2014.

ONLINE

BBC. "Grenada Profile—Timeline." https://www.bbc.com/news/world-latin-america-19596901.

CIA. *The World Factbook*. "Grenada." https://www.cia.gov/library/publications/the-world-factbook/geos/gj.html.

Encyclopaedia Britannica. "Grenada." https://www.britannica.com/place/Grenada.

Government of Grenada. https://www.gov.gd.

Grenada Informer. https://www.thegrenadainformer.com.

Guardian. Grenada archives. https://www.theguardian.com/world/grenada.

Now Grenada. https://www.nowgrenada.com.

BIBLIOGRAPHY

BBC. "Grenada Profile—Timeline." https://www.bbc.com/news/world-latin-america-19596901.

Caribbean Development Bank. "Country Economic Review 2018: Grenada." https://issuu.com/caribank/docs/cdb_economic_brief_2018_-_grenada.

CIA. *The World Factbook.* "Grenada." https://www.cia.gov/library/publications/the-world-factbook/geos/gj.html.

Commonwealth, The. http://thecommonwealth.org.

Encyclopaedia Britannica. "Grenada." https://www.britannica.com/place/Grenada.

Freedom House. "Freedom in the World 2018: Grenada Profile." https://freedomhouse.org/report/freedom-world/2018/grenada.

Garely, Elinor. "Grenada: Poverty or Paradise?" *eTurboNews*, November 4, 2017. https://www.eturbonews.com/169519/grenada-poverty-paradise.

International Monetary Fund. "Grenada: Climate Change Policy Assessment." July 3, 2019. https://www.imf.org/en/Publications/CR/Issues/2019/07/01/Grenada-Climate-Change-Policy-Assessment-47062.

IUCN Red List. "Grenada Dove." https://www.iucnredlist.org/species/22690874/131031811.

Mead, Leila. "Caribbean Ministers Approve Action Plan on Climate-Resilient Health Systems." International Institute for Sustainable Development (ISSD), January 15, 2019. https://sdg.iisd.org/news/caribbean-ministers-approve-action-plan-on-climate-resilient-health-systems.

OSAC. "Barbados & Grenada 2018 Crime & Safety Report." https://www.osac.gov/Content/Report/361e3bc6-3324-44e9-b921-15f4ae5e3230.

Stewart, Stacy R. "Tropical Cyclone Report." National Hurricane Center, National Oceanic and Atmospheric Administration, December 2004, updated 2011. https://www.nhc.noaa.gov/data/tcr/AL092004_Ivan.pdf.

US Department of State. "International Religious Freedom Report 2005 (archived)." https://2009-2017.state.gov/j/drl/rls/irf/2005/51639.htm.

World Atlas. "What Are the Biggest Industries in Grenada?" July 5, 2019. https://www.worldatlas.com/articles/what-are-the-biggest-industries-in-grenada.html.

World Bank. "Transitioning Toward a Blue Economy in Grenada and Other Eastern Caribbean States." May 8, 2018. https://www.worldbank.org/en/results/2018/05/08/transitioning-toward-a-blue-economy-in-grenada-and-other-eastern-caribbean-states.

INDEX

INDEX